Seeking
The Seekers

SEEKING THE SEEKERS

Serving the Hidden Spiritual Quest

PAUL MACLEAN
MICHAEL THOMPSON

Potentials:
A Canadian Ecumenical Centre for the
Development of Ministry & Congregations
Toronto, ON, Canada

Anglican Book Centre
Toronto, Canada

2000
Anglican Book Centre
600 Jarvis Street
Toronto, Ontario
M4Y 2J6

Copyright © 1999 Paul MacLean and Michael Thompson

All rights reserved. No part of this book may be reproduced, stored in a retrieval system, or transmitted, in any form or by any means, electronic, mechanical, photocopying, recording, or otherwise, without the *written permission* of the publisher.

Photo of Michael Thompson by Ken Mulveney.

Cover illustration: the window of Saint Thomas at the cathedral of Bourges

Canadian Cataloguing in Publication Data
MacLean, Paul, 1945–
    Seeking the seekers : serving the hidden spiritual quest

ISBN 1-55126-308-4

1. Church renewal. 2. Church growth.
I. Thompson, Michael James, 1956– . II. Title.

BV600.2.M324 2000   262'.001'7   C99-933100-0

Contents

Acknowledgements 6
The Story Behind This Book 7
There Is Still a Place for the Mainline Churches 15
Change, Community, Faith, and Spirituality 27
Old Churches, New Christians 41
The Discovery Project 79
Appendix 149
Bibliography 158
About the Authors 159

Acknowledgements

We would like to thank the following people for their contribution to this book. First of all, none of it would have been possible without the open sharing of the focus group participants. The team of focus facilitators from St.Cuthbert's entered into The Discovey Project with enthusiasm and a willingness to learn. In the early days, Don Posterski, Leslie Francis, and Kirk Hadaway helped us shape the questions for The Discovery Project. The Program Resources Department of the Diocese of Toronto provided a grant for the project. Ann Tottenham, Mardi Tindal, Bill Lord, and Loren Mead all read the manuscript and provided helpful comments for its revision. Greig Dunn made many improvements in organization and style. Through it all, Robert Maclennan provided unflagging encouragement, helpful suggestions, and some significant improvements in the text.

Many thanks.

The Story Behind This Book

Paul MacLean

There were, as usual, two conversations going on at the same time at the dinner table. My three children, ages nineteen to twenty-six, were arguing with some passion about whether or not faith and belief are necessary parts of belonging to a church. After all, my daughter pointed out, many people are simply seeking a good community to belong to, and they attend a church more from motives of friendship, family, and affiliation than from intense religious belief. On the other hand, her younger brother countered, could a church survive for long if these are the dominant motives of the people who make up its membership? Wouldn't it lose its way and stray from the sources of its life and energy? These thoughts were met with a further argument that perhaps there is a strong spiritual element underlying the search for community, and so the church is an appropriate place for this searching to happen. It has to go beyond comfort in its community to provide challenge and opportunities for spiritual growth.

So the argument went. The second conversation was being carried on by our guests, who were all slightly past the mid-century mark. With somewhat less intensity they were discussing the ideal retirement location and calculating how soon they could get there.

Could this dual conversation be a little parable for the church? Although I'm in the second of these age groups, I'm not interested much in retirement conversations. They don't have the same energy as conversations that are about engagement with life.

This book is about engagement. It is about some churches that engage with people in a new and exciting way. It is about people: some who engage with churches and others who don't. There is, however, in both these groups of people an enormous interest in things spiritual; it's just that one group has found a home for their interest in a church and the other group hasn't. Whether we are talking about churches, about people who have recently joined churches, or about people who haven't, the common thread through it all is energy and engagement.

The energy and engagement come both from individuals and from congregations. In the two research projects that gave rise to this book, we have talked with people who have spiritual motivation. They are representative of a group that has been called "seekers." Some have found their way into a Christian community and others have not. However, the research was not just about individuals who are seekers; it also had to do with understanding congregations that in one way or another seek to "seek the seekers." The congregations, too, have spiritual motivation, and seek to engage people who are beyond the membership boundaries that give any organization its stability.

So, the title of this book, *Seeking the Seekers: Serving the Hidden Spiritual Quest*, refers both to individuals and to congregations, and thereby to the dynamic interplay that occurs when connections are made between the two around questions of faith and what is most significant for daily living.

The experiences that gave rise to this book constitute a story in themselves.

The story of Old Churches, New Christians

For some years I have coordinated a planning team for a monthly eucharist at my local church. The planning principles are that this eucharist is a participatory celebration for all ages, including children and adolescents, that it creates an inclusive community, that it makes use of all the arts (visual, dance, music, drama), and that the music is drawn from folk traditions around the world. This service has been a creative outlet for developing new forms of celebration for people who live in the inner city. It continues to attract a diverse congregation as an alternative offering to the more traditional services of this particular church. Here is an example of a church that is trying to engage with people it wouldn't otherwise be able to reach through the creation of a very energetic experience of worship. It also provides an ongoing experiment from which I continue to learn. I am a participant in a continually developing process of finding new forms of celebration that capture something of the post-modern, unsatisfied yearning for God. From time to time I step out of the stream and ask myself, "What is going on here and why?"

One of the things going on in this particular church is a changing relationship between the experimental and the traditional congregations. After some years of mutual distrust, they are now supportive of each other and take pleasure in seeing the diversity in worship the church is able to offer. The experimental congregation is an example of parallel development within an established church. The traditional congregation, at least for the moment, has come to see the newcomers not as cuckoos in the nest, but as a new source of life and energy.

It was this experience at my local church that led me, during a brief sabbatical period, to formulate some questions and investigate them. What motivates some young adults to join churches, and what motivates churches to make themselves open to seekers? And so I developed a modest research project in which I interviewed groups of young adults, drawn mostly from the baby boom generation, who had recently joined a church. But I was also interested to investigate the churches they joined. What was it about these congregations that attracted and retained new Christians? Are there any conclusions we can draw about the motivating energy of individuals and the responsiveness of organizations? I think there are.

The story of The Discovery Project

The next stage of the story involves the forming of a partnership. My long-time friend, Michael Thompson, was part of a group who reflected on the results of this first research project. The issues raised in the project were ones that had engaged him, both in his parish practice and in his work on a Doctor of Ministry degree. Several years later, his parish devised a creative project to connect with people in the neighbourhood who were interested in spirituality but who did not belong to a church. I was invited to join this project as a consultant.

Two sources of energy connected in this project: a group of congregational leaders prepared to listen beyond the normal boundaries of their church, and a group of people beyond those boundaries who were willing to talk about spirituality. In this second project, we were listening to people who have *not* found the church to be a place that supports their spiritual seeking. What we heard is challenging and creative, with implications both for the life of the congregation and for the seekers whom they interviewed.

Michael's congregation is what used to be called a mainline church. Although mainline churches are anxious about declining membership and participation, most of the effort towards attracting seekers seems to have come from elsewhere. "Elsewhere" has usually meant south of the Canadian border, and the effort has come from churches that could be described as conservative evangelical, pentecostal, or mega-churches. Yet the seekers we were meeting had not been attracted to any of these. We think that this presents a challenge to what Michael has termed the historic-cultural churches. Before we enter a description of the two research projects, we offer some reflections on the church scene and on the particular strengths of the historic-cultural churches in responding to seekers, both those who are willing to join churches and those who aren't.

That's how this book came to be written.

Who is this book for and what can you expect to learn from it?

This book is for people in ordinary churches who are wondering what future the church has. It is for church leaders, both clergy and lay, who care about two things. First, they care about congregations and believe congregations will be around for a long time. They are prepared to think about the future path of development these congregations need to follow in order to be authentic expressions of the Christian gospel in their given context. They believe that the actions they take now are steps along that path. Second, they care about people, whether the people happen to belong to a congregation or not, and they are prepared to listen carefully and learn what energy and questions motivate them. They know that people from outside the boundaries of congregations bring spiritual energy that can give new life and direction to their congregations. As we will say in our conclusion, much of this new life and direction depends upon congregations rediscovering their role as servants in the mission of God for the world.

This is not a "how-to" book. It won't give you the ten steps for creating a successful church. It's a book for people who have come to the conclusion that there aren't any easy answers but who aren't discouraged by this fact.

We hope that you will learn from the discoveries that we have made and the processes by which we made them. We also hope that the reflections and theoretical frameworks that we introduce will be helpful to you in engaging some of the questions that we share in common. As well as telling the story, in the appendix we provide the resources we developed for understanding both people and churches, and we invite you to use or adapt them. Our greatest hope is that we can encourage you to engage in your own process of seeking seekers and serving the hidden spiritual quest.

Don't expect a retirement package.

THERE IS STILL A PLACE FOR THE MAINLINE CHURCHES

Michael Thompson

Guru heartbreak

Every year or two a new guru appears to teach congregations how to grow and prosper. These gurus give lectures, run workshops, write books. Their names are dropped in conversations among church leaders. They have answers: fill your church by changing the music or by developing small groups. They have success stories about leading congregations through the wilderness to the promised land. We leaders decide to follow them. We, too, will turn our churches around. We, too, will catch the vision and courageously advocate the overhaul of our congregations.

But back home from the lecture, reality hits. We try to communicate the vision, and in reply we receive blank stares. What can be wrong? Maybe we ourselves are the problem. If only we had more courage, more conviction, more passion. If only we were prepared to take risks. If only we had the guru's eloquence. We despise ourselves. Or we despise the congregations to which we belong. If only they weren't so pigheaded, so stuck in the past.

But the problem isn't necessarily leaders and it isn't necessarily congregations. It may well be the guru's sales pitch or the package, and it may well be our own readiness to invest heavily in someone else's story.

As the seasons of celebrity come and go, we may discern a pattern of hopes raised by other people's success and dashed by our inability to reproduce that success. "Guru heartbreak" seems almost inevitable when the guru's package is at odds with a congregation's heritage or identity. Even among churches that share a common denominational heritage, theological orientation, or local identity, there are enough differences to make "one-size-fits-all" programs unlikely to take root and flourish.

Finding ourselves in diversity

The Christian church is not a monolith. It contains a variety of approaches, histories, values, theological understandings, and assumptions about people. Within the church, boundaries separate diverse — and sometimes conflicting — "cultures." Crossing those boundaries without taking them seriously is a major reason for "guru heartbreak." When the guru's program package is imposed on an environment where it doesn't fit, it seldom works. When it does work, it reshapes the environment to conform with the assumptions, values, and heritage from which the package is derived.

We are familiar with some of the "cultures" within the church and the boundaries separating them: Roman Catholic and Protestant, conservative and liberal. But today other "cultures" are discernible, each with its own heritage, identity, and program. Four stand out: conservative evangelical, pentecostal/charismatic, mega-churches, and historic-cultural churches.

The historic-cultural churches are those that used to be called "mainstream." They are distinguished by their deep historic roots, reaching back at least to the Reformation, and by their pattern of deep engagement and making common cause with their host culture.

This book is concerned with discovering the vitality in the historic-cultural churches. They are mainstream no longer; in fact, they are marginal to the prevailing culture. In the past, their deep engagement with their host culture has made them at times tragically indistinguishable from its agendas: imposing particular values such as patriarchy and property rights; conquering and colonizing half the world in a mission that was thought to be "civilizing." Now, as they stand to the side of the cultural mainstream, there may yet be value in what remains of their closeness to the culture and their habit of working within it.

Conservative evangelicals, pentecostal-charismatics, and mega-churches have clearly defined cultures and a more or less clearly focused sense of mission. The historic-cultural churches, having lost their identity as cultural forces and their mission focus in converting the heathen in lands afar, are seeking to understand themselves and the role that they might play. They are coming to terms with what Loren Mead has identified as the loss of Christendom — the period of church history that began with the conversion to Christianity of the Roman Emperor Constantine in 313 CE and lasted until perhaps the Second World War. For all those centuries the historic-cultural churches worked in ready collaboration with the dominant social, economic, and political forces.

Perhaps one of the reasons for the appeal of church growth gurus is that they promise a new identity and sense of mission. But the guru's package seldom fits the heritage of the historic-cultural churches and our sense of who we are. If we buy it, we are apt to be abandoning our own story.

My conviction is that the future of historic-cultural congregations lies not in adopting a foreign church "culture" nor in assimilating the program of a church growth guru. Rather, our future lies in identifying the possibilities and challenges in our own historic-cultural tradition, and in working with those possibilities and challenges in the context where we find ourselves.

Before we try to uncover the hidden heritage of the historic-cultural churches, it will be useful to explore the other three strong church "cultures" in order to identify their core mission and to understand their limits.

Conservative evangelical: right belief

The mission of conservative evangelical churches has been, for the most part, the cultivation of right belief. Right belief is often defined as assent to sets of propositions about God, about Jesus as personal saviour, about the inerrancy of scripture, about human sexuality, about the use of alcohol, and so on. The boundary that sets the conservative evangelical church apart from the civic community is propositional belief. Its identity and that of its members is rooted in shared belief in a set of propositions about God. ("Fundamentalism" is the term used to describe one of these sets of propositions.)

By contrast, the historic-cultural churches have a centuries-old heritage, not of differentiation from the prevailing culture, but of making common cause with it. Setting themselves apart by assenting to a set of propositions is unlikely to seem an attractive or even viable alternative to such churches.

Pentecostal-charismatic

If the conservative evangelical churches tend to distinguish themselves by normative propositional belief, pentecostal-charismatic churches tend to distinguish themselves by normative religious experience. For example, it is the official teaching of the Pentecostal Assemblies of Canada that the normative expression of the baptism of the Holy Spirit is "speaking in tongues."

In the charismatic movement, the emphasis on normative religious experience is not codified, but it is nonetheless real. When pentecostalism in the form of the charismatic movement makes incursions into the historic-cultural churches, it is characterized by normative feelings, inner experiences, and outward manifestations of emotional religious experience. It often flourishes by replacing a weakened historic-cultural tradition rather than strengthening it. Churches that turn to pentecostal-charismatic models of renewal often cease to be historic-cultural in anything but name.

The mega-church: growth without history

What everyone notices about mega-churches is that they acquire new members at an amazing rate. For this reason they are immensely attractive as models for leaders in struggling congregations. Some of the new members come from other churches, but, as the mega-church mission directs, many come from among the unchurched.

Mega-churches work best when there is little or no collective memory at the outset. In fact, many of them were founded from scratch and are still in their first generation of senior leadership. Most historic-cultural churches, on the other hand, have an abundance of collective memory: a world of shared meaning, some of it obvious and explicit, some of it hidden and tacit. Things are not just things; more often than not, church furniture, hymn books, and regimental flags are visible reminders of important events and values in the congregations' heritage. Past adversity and shared success, favourite memories of clergy, lay leaders, choir directors, and "characters" — these are the landmarks to which people look for significance. Models of renewal that ignore or underestimate the power of collective memory are unlikely to be useful in historic-cultural congregations. While we can learn from the openness of mega-churches, our openness needs to be compatible with our existing heritage and identity.

A second feature of mega-churches is their regional nature. They tend to exist near the edge of large metropolitan areas and draw both members and seekers from a wide catchment area. There is only one Willow Creek in the Chicago area, only one People's Church in the Greater Toronto Area. The historic-cultural church pattern of smaller local churches is not necessarily less effective. While the mega-church is highly visible and looks big, it stands apart from the communities in which we live, work, and play; smaller local churches stand in the midst of these communities, where collectively they can connect with at least as many, probably more, people than the mega-churches.

Real choices for real churches in the historic-cultural tradition

Enough people in our society are predisposed to a conservative evangelical, charismatic, or soft-rock-and-more approach to religion to ensure that there will always be success stories in those "market segments." But many more people will be left unmoved by these approaches and left out. In the complex web of modern society, no single religious framework can suit everyone, still less dominate the scene. There are other "markets," and other ways to think of the church's relationship with those around us.

The key to renewed vitality for the historic-cultural churches is understanding, valuing, revitalizing, and acting upon our own heritage and identity. Reclaiming and renewing the historic-cultural voice may be a more challenging and uncertain task than appropriating another voice, be it conservative evangelical, charismatic, or mega-church. But the loss of that voice would, without doubt, seriously impoverish the array of resources committed to sharing in God's mission for the world.

The church growth gurus gain authority from the tacit assumption that our choice is limited. Buy the package, or live with a boring, empty church. Embrace an external "culture," substitute someone else's story for our own, or slide down the status quo into oblivion.

There are other choices. Good work is already being done at denominational, regional, and local levels to reconfigure the historic-cultural tradition to present circumstances. The Christendom pattern is behind us; we can no longer make an impact by collaborating with the dominant social, economic, and political forces. But we are rediscovering our capacity to engage the prevailing culture at the local, human level. In cities, towns, villages, neighbourhoods, and rural crossroads across the country, local churches are seeking to re-engage with their local environment.

Renewing the historic-cultural tradition

The new Christians who speak in "Old Churches, New Christians," the first of the two research projects that this book describes, make clear that the historic-cultural churches have something to offer. If that were not so, they would not have become members of historic-cultural congregations. And yet, in the course of "The Discovery Project," the second of the two projects, it became clear that the difference between someone "just inside" and someone "outside," in terms of adherence to a set of beliefs that could be called "orthodox," was often difficult to discern. For many people, whatever draws them into participation in the life of a congregation has little to do with a commonly agreed and comprehensive belief system. What draws them, then? It seems that the church provides a communal and reflective framework for their own quest for meaning, purpose, and commitments. It provides a set of relationships, and a shared celebration of diverse and plural human spiritual experience.

If this profile fits other historic-cultural congregations (and I suspect it fits many — perhaps even the majority), it may provide a clue to the source of vitality in a historic-cultural congregation. Many such congregations are already offering a hospitable environment for the human search for meaning and purpose in community, and many more have the potential to do so.

Both projects revealed the existence of a desire to live a life with depth, a life that makes a difference. Transparent in each of the conversations that make up The Discovery Project is the desire of people to live life with commitment and purpose. This is true even though they are not active members of a church, synagogue, mosque, or temple. What is missing is a setting in which they can openly explore this spiritual dimension in their lives. The historic-cultural church can provide that setting.

Marjorie Suchocki has described the mission of the church as fostering human responsiveness to "the call of God toward the world's well-being." The "discovery" at the heart of The Discovery Project is that the spiritual searching of non-members of the church is congruent with God's call. Here lies the mission of the historic-cultural churches. We can welcome into our churches the human search for meaning, purpose, and lives of commitment, and draw it together with the call of God "toward the world's well-being." We know that God turns to the world in love, seeking human partners and empowering us by the Spirit to heal and renew that world. We are discovering that human beings turn also towards God, asking questions about meaning and purpose and wanting with all their hearts to make a difference.

The challenge for the historic-cultural churches is to find the story of Spirit already present in our own history, identity, and spirituality, and then to probe the mystery of the same Spirit at work in the world around us in the human search for meaning and purpose.

Surfacing the hidden heritage and understanding our mission

There is a historic-cultural heritage. It is different from the mega-church, conservative evangelical, and pentecostal-charismatic "cultures." Without denying the contribution those cultures can make to the body of Christ and the mission of God, we need neither imitate nor do battle with them. Instead, we can discern some of the marks of a renewed historic-cultural heritage:

1. Each human person is fashioned in the image and likeness of God, and is intended to share in God's mission in and for the world.

2. The human desire to make a difference contains the seeds of partnership with God in God's mission in and for the world. The church's responsibility is to foster, interpret, and celebrate that partnership.

3. While we take seriously the power of sin to obscure the image of God and impair the divine-human partnership, we interpret sin as obstacles: obstacles within and around us that hinder our mission partnership with God and block our human capacity to "make a difference."

4. The resources of Spirit — forgiveness, hospitality, liberation — disclosed in Israel and in Jesus are directed towards healing the image of God in human lives and renewing the divine-human partnership.

5. A congregation is not a collection of people who have arrived at the same metaphysical or credal conclusions, or who agree on a normative outward expression of religious experience. It is a hospitable community in and through which people may continue their search and deepen their sense of Spirit and commitment.

6. The spiritual journey cannot proceed without a sense of God's presence within and among those who participate in congregational life. While the historic-cultural heritage is not focused on particular orthodoxies, its heritage of scripture and tradition is an invaluable resource for discerning the presence of God and the leading of the Spirit.

We can learn from the culture, practices, and spirituality of other approaches. The conservative evangelicals' clarity of identity and purpose; the charismatic attentiveness to the Spirit; the mega-church "preferential option" for the unchurched — all these can contribute to our search for renewal.

But as historic-cultural churches, we bring our own heritage into play. Our renewal will happen one congregation at a time as people find the questions with which to engage with the world around them. As we re-examine our mission, The Discovery Project contributes this question for the asking: How can churches build relationships with the church-wary by

- taking seriously their spiritual searching
- honouring their desire to contribute to the life of the world, and
- offering a hospitable environment in which that search can continue and that desire grow and flourish into action?

Change, Community, Faith, and Spirituality

Paul MacLean

"Turning and turning in the widening gyre,/ The falcon cannot hear the falconer;/ Things fall apart, the centre cannot hold" wrote William Butler Yeats in 1921. He gave expression to a deep angst in the human psyche that all of us experience at one time or another. The things falling apart may be in a person's life: a job loss and with it the loss of self-esteem, the death of a loved one and the removal of intimacy, a divorce and a plunge into the unknown. The things falling apart may equally be a social or historical phase of chaos, war, social upheaval, or the rise of totalitarian movements. One thinks of the significant effects on North Americans still living of the Great Depression, the Second World War, the massive social change of the 1960s, and the Vietnam War.

As soon as we began talking with people participating in the two research projects that form the heart of this book, we realized that we were delving into territory where things had fallen apart. By simply raising the subjects of faith and spirituality, we were inviting people to talk about the significant experiences that had formed the core of their being and that lifted them beyond a mundane existence. In a mundane existence things are held together, and we can live life in a more or less orderly, rational fashion. We invited people to reflect on life beyond the mundane, when it had proved inadequate, when their experience wasn't orderly or rational. Most of the people we talked to had put things back together again with varying degrees of competence, but one way or another, one time or another, they had experienced life as irrational and chaotic and therefore knew that another dimension existed, which they were prepared to talk about using the categories of faith and spirituality.

Before entering the two projects and hearing the stories and reflections of the people we interviewed, we offer a framework for understanding and interpreting the data we collected.

Change, liminality, and communitas

William Bridges touched a nerve with his book, *Transitions: Making Sense of Life's Changes*. A further subtitle suggests that the reader will find "strategies for coping with the difficult, painful, and confusing times in your life." It seems that an enormous number of people have experienced traumatic changes and want help understanding and coping with these changes, so much so that the book has been in print for twenty years and remains a best seller. In this book, Bridges popularizes an approach to change that has been developed by the anthropologist, Victor Turner, especially in his book *The Ritual Process: Structure and Anti-Structure*.

Turner, too, was interested in understanding the transitions in people's lives. He saw that in traditional societies people passed through major changes such as birth, achieving manhood and womanhood, marriage, change in social status and location, sickness, and death. In each case there were rituals that involved the whole community to see the individuals through these transitions. They passed from one state of being that was settled, ordered, and rational into a time of being unsettled and disoriented, and then into a new and changed state in which order and relationships were restored. The rituals are transition rites, or rites of passage, that give expression to and carry the individuals through the stages of the transition.

He sees three stages to any transition: separation, liminality, and reaggregation. In the first stage people are separated from their social environment and in the process stripped of their identity. They enter the liminal condition (from *limen*, the Latin for threshold) in which their state becomes highly ambiguous, neither here nor there, betwixt and between. After a time spent in this condition they are reintegrated into society at a higher or lower status. In our society a person who becomes prime minister achieves a higher status through the uncertain, liminal process of election, and a person who goes to jail ends in the degraded society and status of prison by way of the uncertain, liminal process of arrest and trial.

Although Turner began with observations of transitions in traditional societies, he thought that much the same three-stage pattern could be applied to Western societies as the two examples above suggest. We may have lost the rituals that speak to the whole of society and give meaning to the changes we experience; nonetheless, in any significant life change we experience the stages in all their power: a sense of loss and separation from a secure and rational existence, an entry into a highly ambiguous state, and reintegration into society as a changed person. The significant life changes of Western society are not confined to the ordered pattern of a normal life span of birth through death. They are also brought about by social events and conditions such as economic upheaval and social reorganization that are experienced as catastrophic to individuals.

Turner was not content to observe individuals going through transition. Organizations and whole societies go through change as well. They, too, pass from a settled and structured phase through a time of great uncertainty into another state of stability. One of the best examples of this type of transition is the 1960s, a time "when mountains were moving," to use a phrase from Wade Clark Roof's study of the spiritual quests of baby boomers, *A Generation of Seekers*.

We are familiar with and know how to describe the structured phase of our social existence with its social differentiation and hierarchies, complexity, order, and stability. To survive in this social condition, a person needs to find out where they fit, and to know that position and all its relationships well. Technical knowledge is valued highly, but it isn't necessary to know the big picture. People are defined by class, money, title, and status. This is the mundane world of normal existence in which life is fairly predictable and time is measured in hours, days, and years.

The liminal condition is, by contrast, almost impossible to describe. It is everything the structured state is not: betwixt and between, uncertain, ambiguous, out of time. It is best expressed in metaphor: darkness, anonymity, the womb, protean. Bridges calls this "the neutral zone," a time when all the daily mechanisms for getting through life and all the symbols through which life gained meaning are thrown into doubt. In our post-modern world,

> we have abandoned a whole system of dealing with the neutral zone through ritual, and we have tried to deal with personal change as though it were a matter of some kind of readjustment. In so doing, we have lost any way of making sense out of the lostness and the confusion that we encounter when we have gone through disengagement or disenchantment or disidentification. We are like Alice at the bottom of the rabbit hole, muttering, "It'll be no use putting their heads down and saying, 'Come up again, dear!' I shall only look up and say, 'Who am I, then?' Tell me that first, and then, if I like being that person, I'll come up: if not, I'll stay down here till I'm somebody else — but, oh dear!" cried Alice, with a sudden burst of tears, "I do wish they would put their heads down! I am so very tired of being all alone here!" [pp. 130–131]

People who are in the liminal condition often have a deep need for what Turner calls communitas and seek it out. Communitas is similar to what we often mean by community, but it suggests bonds between people that are far more intense. It is not an unstructured state, but it is a structure in which everyone is treated as an equal and hierarchies are flattened. People enter into I-Thou relationships rather than relationships based on status and position. They feel as if they know and are known. Spiritual wisdom that connects the individual to a cosmic purpose is more highly valued than technical knowledge. The world is viewed as essentially sacred and simple, rather than secular and complex. There is a sense of spontaneity and intense community. People live in the eternal now, which transcends the inherent conflicts and contradictions of life in the mundane social system. People will make enormous sacrifices for what they perceive to be the common good. They also give total obedience to the leaders of these expressions of communitas, who guide their followers for good or ill.

For an example one only needs to think of the communitas that characterized the birth of Christianity and that had its origins in the highly liminal leadership of Jesus. Liminal experiences and the communitas that flows from them are at the foundation of every religious movement and are also found in the arts. Ironically, in order to survive over time, these movements need to develop structure, and so they pass into another phase while trying to retain the radioactive potency of the founder's spirit.

I have spent some time elaborating the concepts of change, the stages of transition, the liminal condition, and communitas because I believe these concepts give us a framework for understanding the experiences that our interviewees brought and the characteristics of the relationships in community that they valued.

We can use these concepts not only to understand the experiences of individuals, but also to understand our churches better. Churches exist on a continuum with stability and hierarchy at one end and the spontaneous movement of the Spirit at the other. Both influences are usually at work within the same congregation. In times of significant and irreversible change, it is possible for churches to enter the liminal condition and develop intense communities of faith.

Baby boomers

Most of the interviewees in the two projects were from the baby boom generation; that is, they were born between 1946 and 1964. We know that this group comprises about one-third of the Canadian population, and much time has been spent analyzing them, usually for marketing purposes. When compared with other age groupings in our society, they have very distinctive attitudes and values, especially when it comes to faith, spirituality, and organized religion. Although life stage of course has some influence on the way people think and feel about life, there is much more to this generation's distinctiveness than life stage.

To understand these attitudes and values we need to pay attention to the great social influences that were exerted on the baby boomers during their formative years of late adolescence and early adulthood. The greatest single influence that has turned the baby boomers into "a generation of seekers" was the radical social and political upheaval of the sixties. This was a liminal time in which the social order was challenged, often violently, and alternative communities and lifestyles became the order of the day. Whether they embraced this upheaval with all their being or turned away in horror, the baby boomers were shaped by the events of the sixties into who they are, especially in their values and their attitudes to spirituality and religion. This is particularly evident in the interviewees who saw spirituality in intensely personal terms. However, the themes of social justice, of suspicion of social institutions, of ecological concern, and identification with nature also have their origin in the sixties, and they have a profound spiritual dimension.

Consider some of the features of the collective identity of baby boomers that will help us deepen our understanding of these interviews.

1. Baby boomers came of age at a time of expanding horizons, increased choices, and optimistic dreams. It was also a time of disillusionments and disappointments. Their view came to be that personal choice, not tradition, determines action, and this view is expressed as much in the realm of spirituality and religion as it is in their search for personal fulfilment in the world of work.

2. For them and for their children religion and spiritual exploration are primarily about the search for meaning in life. Baby boomers are now approaching mid-life, a time when there is often an increased capacity for growth and maturity and a time when the contemplation of mortality can lead to a heightened sensitivity to spiritual concerns.

3. Traditional religion was often rejected in the 1960s not only for its impersonal rituals and its inability to connect with life issues, but also for its complicity with bourgeois values. It wasn't that baby boomers rejected religion; it was that

they went through a spiritual crisis in which they saw the inherited institutional forms of religion denying spiritual values.

4. Along with the reemergence of spirituality as a subject of great interest, there is also a high degree of religious and cultural pluralism and multilayered belief and practice. Consequently, it is common for people in the baby boom generation to piece together a personal pastiche from diverse sources that "works for them," as they try to make some sense out of life and find a pathway through it. This is just as true for those who join churches as it is for those who don't.

These four points have been summarized from Wade Clark Roof's excellent book, *A Generation of Seekers: The Spiritual Journeys of the Baby Boom Generation*. He concludes by saying, "In a very basic sense, religion itself was never the problem, only social forms of religion that stifle the human spirit."

Faith and spirituality

Having looked at a theory of change that encompasses both the social and the personal, and a phase of social change that had a profound effect on shaping the attitudes and values of baby boomers, we now turn to the two words that were the starting point for people to describe life beyond mundane existence, a life that had about it traces and hints of liminality.

The two research projects we have combined in this book may seem quite dissimilar on the surface. The one gathered groups of people who had recently joined a church. The other deliberately sought out people who had shown no intention of even participating in any aspect of church life. With the first project we may expect to find people who have an enthusiasm for the congregations they have joined and a centre in the church for meaning and purpose in their lives. The second project deliberately gathers people who are wary about churches, who may indeed care about personal purpose and meaning, but who do not find a home for this search within institutional religion. What could these two groups possibly have in common?

The answer to this question is to be found in what we believe to be the common ground for people who are on a spiritual search, whether this search leads them to join a congregation or whether it carries with it a deep suspicion of any form of organized religion. The common ground is a quest for personal meaning, a willingness to wrestle with questions of ultimate concern such as birth and death, good and evil, a desire to orient one's life around certain values and to make a difference in the world, and an openness to the transcendent. To undertake this quest means almost certainly that a person has found the mundane, predictable world to be inadequate and has been touched by those elements of human experience that are extraordinary and mysterious and that are characteristic of the liminal condition and communitas.

Although the terms "faith" and "spirituality" are not identical, the word most readily understood through which to enter this common ground is, for those belonging to a church, "faith," while the equivalent entry word for the non-religious is "spirituality." Both these terms require a little explanation.

We used the term "faith" in the Old Churches, New Christians project in the sense that it is employed by James Fowler in his book *Stages of Faith*. Fowler is drawing on the work of his mentor, Wilfred Cantwell Smith, who describes faith as "deeper and more personal than religion," or to use Paul Tillich's phrase, "the expression of a person's ultimate concern." Smith goes on to say that human beings are "sustained by faith and knit into communities of faith."

Faith is to be distinguished from religion and belief. Religion is the accumulated tradition of the many and varied expressions of the faith of people in the past. It typically comprises sacred texts, liturgies, history, theology, art, music, and dance. Religion is organized, continuous, and cumulative; it preserves and presents a living tradition. It depends for its life on new expressions of faith in every age. It is more objective than faith, but less experiential. In an ideal situation faith would continue to nourish religion by its search for transcendent value and power, while religion would give form and direction to this search. However, we are far from such an ideal in our own time when many people genuinely search for faith outside the established religious traditions. At any rate, faith and religion have much the same symbiotic relationship as the liminal and structured phases of society in Turner's description.

Faith is also different from belief, at least as the word "belief" has come to be used in its modern sense. When belief occurs in the Bible or in a creed of the church, "I believe" denotes an act and orientation of the heart and will. It's like saying, "I'll give everything for you." By contrast, the modern sense of belief is of a proposition that is held by the believer to be true, with the assumption that this proposition may just as easily be false. "He believes such and such, and he may well be wrong." So we talk of a set of beliefs and mean something very different from the alignment of our wills and hearts that accompanies our search for transcendent value and meaning.

We think that "faith" is a term that allows new Christians to enter the common ground, and to speak of their experiences of spiritual search and discovery without using the full interpretative framework provided by Christian theology. However, it is this very framework that creates a barrier for those spiritual seekers who have not found a home within the Christian tradition. Faith is not an entry word for those outside the church. Despite our attempts to resurrect and redefine it, faith, for those outside the church, carries with it a sense of arrival, certainty, and belonging that does not fit with their experience. While spirituality is not an equivalent term, it does convey a transcendent dimension, suggesting that there are profound connecting points between the aspirations and achievements of the human spirit and the mysterious source of purpose, power, and creativity we Christians name as "Spirit."

"Faith" and "spirituality" are two entry words into a common ground of search for meaning and purpose in life. We explored this ground by asking questions: What experiences have shaped your life and how? Thinking of these experiences, what are some words or phrases you would use to describe your experience of faith? What makes life worth living for you? What do you value most and why? What are the relationships that are most important for you? What difference do you want your life to make, and to whom? What are the visual images that you associate with spirituality? What accomplishments do you celebrate and how? What issues lie unresolved? What supports and what hinders the life of the spirit? Is there a community that supports you in your spiritual search and development? Would you invite your friends to come?

We didn't ask all these questions of all the people we interviewed. We chose from among them and rephrased many, picking out and adapting for each context. Taken together, these questions indicate the ground of meaning, purpose, hope, and energy that is common both to people who describe their spiritual journey in terms of faith and to those who don't. Where the language of organized religion creates barriers, we need to go deeper and find new words in order to have these important conversations. The conversations are about faith, spirituality, and the life experiences that have produced a quest for meaning that cannot be satisfied by the mundane, predictable world and its structured categories. They are conversations worth having.

OLD CHURCHES, NEW CHRISTIANS

Paul MacLean

Why do some young adults join some congregations?

Young adults in their mid to late thirties are noticeably absent from the age profile of the historic protestant denominations in Canada. This age group, the last gasp of the baby boomer generation, belongs to the largest age cohort in our population.

Some of them do find their way into churches, either for the first time or after a prolonged absence. These people are worth paying attention to. What motivates them to come? What have they found in the particular Christian community to which they have attached themselves and not in another? Maybe churches can learn something from people who have just come to faith from a background that has little or no previous experience of the church.

People in their thirties are at a stage in life when the concerns and issues with which they are dealing have a readily identifiable religious or spiritual dimension. Traditionally, the churches have easily connected with their concerns: settling into a career, establishing bonds of intimacy, raising a family. However, research into the values and norms of the baby boom generation shows that this group has radically different views and modes of behaviour from previous generations and also from more recent ones. We can't assume that there will be a natural fit between the spiritual needs arising out of their experience and the religious ethos of a particular church, especially when churches are dominated by an older generation generally out of touch with young adults.

So the questions are worth pursuing: why do some young adults, without previous church experience, find their way into some congregations? What is there in the life and leadership of these congregations that makes them attractive to young adults? If we can begin to answer these questions, we will have a better chance of identifying the points in people's lives when the church can be of service to them, and the ways in which the church can open itself to them.

By now we are well aware of those churches — conservative evangelical, pentecostal-charismatic, or mega-church — whose whole ministry is focused on attracting young adults and creating disciples. Although there is much to be learned from these churches, most of the congregations of the historic-cultural churches are not in a position to focus so narrowly on one segment of the population. The challenge for them is to encounter, attract, and serve new Christians in their spiritual journeys.

What We Did

In my study project, "Old Churches, New Christians," I began by identifying a few churches that were attracting young adults. Since I was working at the time for the national program of the Anglican Church of Canada and had very limited time available for the project, I decided to reduce the variables by contacting only Anglican churches.

I set up focus group interviews at these churches, trying to limit the membership of the groups to new Christians. This proved to be difficult because most of the self-identified "new Christians" had, in fact, some previous experience of the church, usually in childhood. For the second part of the inquiry I visited the churches at least once, attending a service of worship as close to "normal" as possible, talking to people afterwards, and generally picking up what information I could from a two-hour visit. Finally, I decided to interview one group of self-identified non-Christians as a foil to my main sources of information.

In developing a question instrument for the interviews, I wanted to begin with significant events in the lives of the young adults rather than with the meaning that these events had inevitably acquired through association with organized religion. I used the term "faith experiences," following the distinction made between "faith" and "belief" by Wilfred Cantwell Smith and James Fowler. Faith is experiential, while belief is the assent we give to a religious tradition as expressed in creeds, scriptures, liturgy, dogma, and so on. In Fowler's terms, faith has to do with "the centres of value and power that sustain our lives." Everyone experiences faith although not everyone would espouse a belief. At the beginning of each interview, I made this distinction in order to give people permission to locate religious or spiritual experiences outside as well as inside the church setting.

I also developed a point of view or perspective around which to gather information and later analyze it. Since I am interested in the rituals and symbols by which people make collective meaning in their lives, I tried to discern the rituals and symbols that made connections between the new Christians and their congregations. And I was also working with the concept of liminality: that at certain times in our lives, we stand on thresholds, feeling somewhat ill at ease and seeking meaning and direction.

I recorded and transcribed each focus group interview, made my observations and analysis, and then turned to a description of the congregation to which the group belonged. I was trying to discover the links between the individuals and the congregation, paying particular attention to the evidence the congregations presented for connecting with significant events in the lives of the young adults.

My interest in all this is to help the church to understand the spiritual search that brings some people into the church and keeps others out. I am convinced that the way forward is not to find the right church growth guru and start the right program or the right new-style, seeker-friendly church services. The way forward is to engage in the dynamic interplay between the church and its social context.

The focus group

The typical focus group interview lasted about ninety minutes. It had anywhere from five to twelve participants, many of whom were already well acquainted with each other. Confidentiality was assured, and participants were told they didn't have to reveal anything they felt uncomfortable about.

Although focus group interviews usually encourage discussion among participants, I did not do so. Since the questions mostly had to do with personal experience, they were not debatable. I would ask a question, and then each person in the group had the opportunity to respond without comment from the others. We would then pass on to the next question. The result in a group is different than in an individual interview because an atmosphere of respectful listening develops. Experiences, ideas, and opinions are not challenged, but they do stimulate reflection in other members of the group, so that the net effect is a single conversation rather than of a random collection of unrelated thoughts. People tend to relate their experiences and reflections to what they have heard others say, noting contrasts and similarities. By the end of the focus group, interaction was taking place with some frequency. We always ended with some evaluation of the interview.

The questions

1. Describe a significant event in your own life.

By *significant*, I meant something that had enduring meaning, especially if that meaning wasn't fully evident either at the time of the event or on later reflection. An event is something that actually happened, although the time frame in which it happened could vary from a few moments to years. By using the term *significant*, I was introducing the idea of symbol, searching for those experiences that held deep meaning for people.

2. Find a word or phrase that captures the elements or factors of faith in the event.

I encouraged participants to use language that someone not familiar with the church could understand. Whereas the first question gave rise to stories, this question was designed to elicit a few evocative images and metaphors.

3. Did you change in any ways as a result of the significant event?

I asked people to reflect on the "before" and the "after," and then to see what they had given up and what they had gained.

4. What role did the congregation play in your faith development?

I asked what they considered to be the most meaningful aspect of congregational life for them. In a few instances, I asked about the challenges people were currently facing. Did their congregation have any meaningful role in helping them to meet these challenges?

5. Would you invite others to come to your congregation? Why or why not?

New Christians: Experiences of Faith and Finding Meaning

Significant events

Death

The events that people identified were all experiences of transition — liminal or threshold events: death, divorce, marriage, birth, moving to a new home. The events may not have been remarkable in themselves, but in their significance they had been life-changing, and the interviewees continued to reflect on the path their lives had taken because of them.

Typically, when death was mentioned it was the death of a very important figure in the person's life: a parent, grandparent, or very close friend. So the significance lay not just in the fact of death, but in the loss of someone who had been central to the formation of the person's identity.

Sometimes the death resulted, even for a person who had had little exposure to religion, in a remarkable and life-changing encounter with God: "At the ... funeral I felt God speaking to me: 'You don't need to be like her.' Suddenly I had the clarity of seeing her and her life, and seeing that I had the opportunity to do something totally different and to break the pattern. You evaluate your own life when you see someone else's life finished." Sometimes the death shattered what faith was there: "I turned away from God because of his injustice." Yet continued reflection altered this person's initial experience: "Now I realize that life is for learning. I have a new attitude. Christ is the central figure in my life." Sometimes the church provided the needed support: "A dear friend of mine died. I felt shattered and in pain. I prayed and had an experience of deep peace. It was a remarkable event. I returned to church when I felt lonely."

Marriage

Increasingly, people in our society do not seek out a church for rites of passage. Yet marriage and birth, like death, are still significant events that for many people have a religious or spiritual dimension. Often we see that there is much more going on than a wedding or a baptism in church.

One interviewee described "shopping around" for a church to get married in, seeking a person and an organization that would take seriously the depth of her decision to marry, which she couldn't articulate. "Every one of the ministers except [the rector of a particular church] said, 'When do you want your wedding?' They didn't care about why we were getting married. The first thing [the rector] said was, 'I know this is a nice church, and if you want to get married because of that you might as well leave right now.' He started talking and I thought, 'This is really cool.' The other thing I liked is that he is married and has kids, so he knows what he is talking about. If we had just gone [to a church] to get married, I swear I would have never gone back." For her, the barriers were broken down by a pastor who connected the church's rituals with her real life experiences: "The priest explained the marriage vows in reality-type language, not 'higher' church language. Now I feel completeness ... When you go to church you're labelled as a Bible thumper or whatever. When we go to church it's neat. You feel better when things are explained in natural language. You don't feel intimidated."

For some people, marriage was a symbol for addressing changes that reached into every corner of their lives: "I never knew what I wanted to do with my life. I started to play with computers and now I'm teaching others. But I became a different person when we got married. I became responsible. I had never been responsible." For this person, the church congregation took on a profound symbolic importance as the focus of his new-found purpose in life: "The priest was so friendly and understanding, and when he was on hand for marriage counselling, I knew that this was the place I wanted to be even though I was never a church person... For some reason this guy changed us, but it wasn't just him. The people in the church would come and talk to you."

For another person, too, talk of marriage led him beyond the merely intellectual sphere into an encounter with faith: "The church was the building at the end of the street that never had enough money. I was very interested in physics and knew that the world was very complex. I went to churches searching for answers, but there was nothing there to find. Then I was invited to a marriage encounter weekend. That was a turning point. There was no talk of money. Everyone was very loving and friendly. I thought, 'This is what church should be like.'"

Baptism and the raising of children

Like marriage, the birth and raising of children do not necessarily lead to the church. They may, in fact, lead to conflict with what are perceived to be the church's values: "Back in the old days the pressure was on the parents in the light of baptism and the accepted norms. There's something I fought against in that decision and this forced me away from the church. But I knew there was emptiness and loneliness...[When I was considering the baptism of a child born years later than his sibling,] the rector talked about … how they were redirecting their focus back to the roots of Christianity.…This was opposed to my thinking of the church as mostly a hierarchy and the beliefs in which I had been raised up." The phrase "emptiness and loneliness" is a clue that a deeper level has been touched. Equally significant is the rejection of hierarchy. An organization dependent on structure and oppressive authority isn't going to fill the void. In some way the priest's explanation of the early church's dynamic vision of baptism was able to connect with this person's experience of children and with his belief in a more egalitarian family structure.

Other people could not take the step of having their children baptized until they were assured that the congregation would fill their need for a sense of belonging.

"I always felt very happy in the church, [but] when I moved to southern Ontario, it was an extreme change of environment and completely different way of life. I felt a great loss of community, so I just gave up. I tried to go to church, but all the time nobody would talk to me and I would just sit there. I didn't have my children baptized." However, at a new church, "I was welcomed the moment I came in. Two of my children have been baptized here. I feel access to a community that I lost." This baptism wasn't simply a church event. It also signified an important change in place and a commitment to a new community.

Separation

Not all the stories that the interviewees told were happy. "My husband and I separated this spring. This changed my view of my life path. Before, I always knew where I was going, but this sort of turned everything inside out of me. My life was totally unpredictable. Part of me was torn out, destroyed, missing, questioning everything, everything could fall apart." The person who told this story had belonged to a church as a child and adolescent, but found both the church and her faith inadequate to adult life. Her main support was a group of friends, but even these people had little sense of the agony she was going through. With the loss of her primary, intimate relationship, she was facing the abyss.

Other events

Other people told of significant events where nature symbolism carried associations of peace and deep, enduring relationship. Still others told of how music brought stability and a sense of personal order to a life of chaos. "Music is like the sacraments. It's something that makes you remember and helps you understand your faith. I think it's the same one-on-one sense you have when you go to the altar to take your communion."

All the interviewees discovered that faith is found in every part of life, not just in the church, and that it has touched all of their lives, usually with considerable intensity. The significant event was the catalyst for a change that upset the order of their lives and made space for a new and dynamic force that imparted purpose and meaning to life.

Factors of faith

The invitation to find a word or phrase that encapsulated some of the key elements of the significant event and that would be accessible to people unfamiliar with religious or church-related vocabulary proved to be a challenge for some people. They had found it difficult to explain their new church commitment to their non-church-going friends. They knew they were regarded as "religious nuts" because of their involvement in the church, and they had been unsuccessful in making sense of their faith to others who didn't have the experience. "You had to have been there," was the rule that seemed to apply. "I can explain only to people who understand."

Others rose to the challenge, and spoke of their significant events in images that suggest four stages in a process: disintegration, movement to faith and trust, personal reintegration, and commitment to community.

In the stage of disintegration, life seems to be falling apart and none of the old certainties apply. The result is fear, loss, confusion, anger, and depression — "questioning everything, in a pit filled with anger."

In the stage of faith and trust, the source of this new-found trust for most of the interviewees is God. The result is profound thankfulness for God's role in bringing peace and happiness to their lives. Loneliness, abandonment, isolation, emptiness, and the feeling of being lost in a maze or black hole, give way to a sense of gift and blessing, which is shared with others. God is the confidant and guide in a stressful life, the security that allows risk-taking and continuous learning.

Reintegration feels like peace, comfort, completion, release from judgement, the opposite of depression. It is like being pushed to be different person, though still with the fear of falling back.

This new condition of faith, trust, and personal reintegration is not only personal. It also includes joining a community that is connected by strong bonds, like a family; in fact, it is often difficult to separate the new condition from belonging to the community. People's lives revolve around the congregation and what they do together. The congregation provides check points — the big picture — against which to evaluate one's own personal journey.

Role of the congregation

Asked what role the congregation had played in their faith development, people spoke of the beliefs and values of the congregation, the opportunities for learning, and the sense of community.

Beliefs and values of the congregation

One focus group thought that their church stood for something, that there was a core of belief in the life of the congregation that could be traced to the Bible. Furthermore, they said the people in the congregation were sincere in their belief and had basic values that were shared by all who came. Yet standing for something did not compromise individual freedom or induce stifling conformity; on the contrary, there was considerable latitude for personal expression and an emphasis on having fun together. The sense of committed friendship continued outside the church context, and for many people the groups they joined at church became their primary source of community.

Opportunities for learning

Other people identified learning opportunities available through some of the more traditional programs of the church, such as Sunday school or Bible studies.

One congregation had a highly intentional program of small groups in which people could explore their faith, and one participant noted, "It has given me a chance to search and explore;

it's not taken for granted that you know anything. You can start from square one. Belief is not assumed. The approach is non-threatening. This is not a competition. The whole approach is education-based and therefore motivational. They talk to you on an equal basis, like you're real people."

These responses contain important insights into the interaction between an individual's faith development and the environment provided by the larger faith community. As in the parable of the labourers in the vineyard, everyone is treated equally and with respect, no matter at what point they become aware that they are on a spiritual journey. The image of "searching and exploring" implies that considerable space and latitude are given. But the community is not without direction, and this is provided by the learning opportunities. People may be in very different places on their faith journeys, but they have the journey in common. And the learning they speak of is not the content-oriented education of a theological course or of a structured organization where it is necessary to know complex norms, history, rituals, and regulations in order to participate. Learning arises from the issues brought by the participants and is holistic in nature.

Sense of community

The focus group at a church in an international city had developed strong bonds of friendship through the church. They were mostly young, single adults who had come to the city to work or study for a few years. They were energetic and transient; and they had clearly defined, immediate needs for belonging. In the focus group at another church, the interviewees described how the congregation supported the bonds of marriage and created a context for the more intimate relationships to flourish.

In some congregations small groups form that become the primary communities for their members, particularly single, young adults. These groups are intense. The sharing that takes place in them around the development of faith leads to the spending of much social time together. The groups meet strong needs for friendship and belonging. In other congregations the level of intensity is lower and the groups are more diffuse, but the bonds are intricate and strong because faith development and the forming of intimate relationships are bound together.

Inviting others to join the congregation

Since the interviewees' feelings about their congregations were so positive, the response to the question, "Surely this is a congregation you would have no hesitation inviting a friend to?" came as a surprise. There was both hesitation and disagreement. There was great respect for the positions taken by others. Some thought that it was right to bring the non-Christian to church, but others were less sure. Perhaps it was better first to bring Christian faith to someone's problem and afterwards to issue an invitation. One has to be open to the time in people's lives when they are looking for welcome, meaning, and love. Only then will an invitation be appropriate. Even then, the experience of congregational worship is not enough in itself to sustain the life of faith.

Those already in the church asked themselves whether those outside the church are really uninterested in religious questions about significance and meaning or just uninterested in organized religion. Would they be open to discussing questions of faith and religious experience in a setting of exploration and acceptance, such as the participants themselves found so helpful?

Those who did not belong to a church confirmed this reticence. They were not interested in exploring faith within the context of organized religion, although they did admit to reflecting on the spiritual dimension of life: "I would say that a person can't be whole unless there is a spiritual component that they've accepted within themselves. It's different for every person. It's dangerous for religious movements to dictate what that spirituality should be ... I have a hard time understanding people that don't question theological events. I can't relate to the Bible because it tells stories that have been proven to be totally unrealistic." Someone else commented: "We're here for each other. When we're gone, we're gone. People's purpose in life is to make other people's lives all the better. It's not that there's no meaning to life, but the mystery is not up there. What's important is each and every one of us."

For these people, spirituality is a matter of personal interpretation. It should not be mediated by a religious organization because the organization will either distort the spiritual dimension of life or will make irrational demands for obedience that diminish a person's intellectual capacities for discernment. Meaning and purpose are found in the here and now, and spiritual significance, in human beings and their relationships.

The cleavage is clear between those who belong to a faith community and those who don't. Although they may have in common a belief in the spiritual dimension of human relationships, they part company in identifying meaning, purpose, and mystery with God.

OLD CHURCHES: CONNECTING WITH NEW CHRISTIANS

Churches and their identity: what attracts young adults with little Christian memory?

At this point we shift from listening to the faith stories of individuals to looking at snapshots of the churches they joined so that we can ask, "Is there anything distinctive about these 'old churches' that makes them attractive to adults who are discovering faith for the first time?" In particular, we need to look for ways in which these congregations were able to connect with the interviewees' significant events and their experience of being in a liminal state.

There is something deeper about a congregation than its program. We got a sense of this earlier when people spoke of their church as standing for something and of its members, despite their diversity, sharing common values such as mutual love, friendship, a sense of community, and a love of learning. This deeper aspect of a congregation is its identity.

The program of a congregation is, to a certain extent, the outward expression of its identity. Programs are ways in which a congregation puts its organized energies into what it sees as most important for its life and development. However, we can also find examples of apparently good programs that just don't seem to work. Very often this is because the program doesn't fit with the identity of the congregation.

If we are going to look deeper into how old churches connect with new Christians, we need to know something about the possibilities and limitations contained in these churches' identities.

In her chapter "Culture and Identity in the Congregation" in the book *Studying Congregations,* Nancy Ammerman lists six elements that go into observing and interpreting the identity of a congregation:

- its central and predictable rituals, especially those that give access to the liminal times in members' lives
- its most important activities that shape its members
- its key symbols: objects, people, and events that carry the meaning of the group
- its style of relationships that best capture the values of the congregation
- its stories and essential myths
- its core beliefs and ideas

In considering the relationship between a church's identity and those who don't count themselves among its members, the question is not simply, How can a church attract new people? It is, What does this church have to offer that is worthwhile? What is worthwhile is a church's particular expression of faith and how it makes that faith available to people. Furthermore, a church, like an individual, is constantly changing and developing its identity. In a vibrant church the elements that make up its identity and make it "worthwhile" do not come across as static but as dynamic and attractive.

Observing congregations

How do we discover a congregation's identity? Very often members may be quite oblivious to certain aspects of their congregational identity, such as the symbolic effect of their church's furnishing (until someone wants to make a change). On the other hand, any newcomer to a church will immediately be able to say a fair amount about the congregation's identity. Did it feel warm and welcoming, or stiff and formal? Did the liturgical leader seem to be engaged or just going through the motions? Did the newcomer feel as though it would be possible to fit in? The impressions are inevitably framed in terms of certain biases and expectations that the newcomer brings. I have yet to meet a congregation that wouldn't describe itself as friendly, warm, and welcoming; but sometimes a newcomer may find it difficult to break through the formidable crust to find the warm bread inside.

I have developed a simple, three-part way of being a participant/observer in congregations:

Attend a normal Sunday service and any connected social activity

> You can learn a lot about nearly every aspect of congregational identity through observing and participating in a single service of worship, which is a powerful, symbolic focus of its life. Often hundreds of hours have gone into its preparation, and these hours represent an investment of energy and value that is usually transparently evident.

Pick up general information about congregational life from informal but directed conversation and other sources

> A few informal conversations, reading the congregational literature and notices, and observing social interaction

will usually reveal most of the obvious data about the communities that gather under the banner of the congregation, and something about their relation and attitude to the surrounding neighbourhood and the wider context.

Interview a few members

To have the privilege of a few focused interviews gives another unique window into the congregation's identity. Here one learns about congregational history, myth, and story through the lens of particular individuals. Usually each individual gives two viewpoints, which are woven inextricably together: a unique perspective that only he or she can give, and a representation of the common story insofar as it has been learned and integrated. This third source of information lends a richness and depth that is otherwise difficult to achieve.

In trying to understand the program and identity of the churches I visited, I was interested in understanding how some churches could attract and assimilate the people we are calling spiritual seekers.

- Is the attraction planned and by intention, or does it just happen?
- How are new people integrated? Do they simply fit in, or do they pose a challenge to the status quo?
- How elastic and expansive is the identity of a congregation, and where does it set up boundaries regarding belief, behaviour, and values?

Four churches, four identities

Church one: energy from below

The first church I visited is a joint chaplaincy to British Anglicans and American Episcopalians in Europe. Therefore its supposed constituency is English-speaking expatriates who are already members of the Anglican Church and who seek to worship in familiar surroundings and liturgy while living abroad. But the reality is quite different. While the congregation includes this group, it also encompasses new Christians, members of various branches of the Dutch Reformed tradition, people for whom English is a second or third language, and many visitors.

The outward symbols of the church are very British. The Union Jack flies on the flagpole. The clergy are dressed as for an English cathedral service of fifty years ago. The hymns are all British. The Sunday morning ethos is moderate British evangelical, although there is a more emotional service with a charismatic flavour in the evening.

On the other hand, there is another powerful strain in this church's identity that runs counter to the dominant symbol system. It may best be described as a free-wheeling, alternative community focused in a group significantly called "the aliens." It consists of young adults who have come from other countries to work or study in the city, and who find themselves labelled as aliens by the host country. Rather than adopt the very British symbols of the congregation as a way of giving themselves an identity, the aliens take on the solidarity of stateless outcasts and develop strong interpersonal bonds through shared experiences.

The clergy, although part of the British identity of the church, connect to this group of young adults through genuine friendliness. There are organized activities and informal pastoral care by which the church shows its desire to minister to their needs for friendship, practical assistance, and belonging. These needs are all the more pronounced because of the transitory lifestyle of many of these young adults. Their loyalty and gratitude are equally strong. The experience of community continues throughout the week in many shared activities.

There seems to be no open conflict between the somewhat staid ethos characteristic of the British evangelical tradition and this more fluid and dynamic experience of the "alien" community. There is, however, a certain amount of disagreement and grumbling over music, and this may be an expression of the clash between symbols and values. The emotional music of the charismatic service is more in keeping with the experience of intense community among young adults, and this service is clearly designed to appeal to this group. However, the music is often trite, and so comes under some criticism from the very people it is intended for. On occasion, the evening service is planned entirely by the young adults, and at these times the intense community developed in the small groups finds liturgical expression.

Church two: living between two worlds

The church building is a freshly renovated white frame structure set within a graveyard. It dates from 1839. To one side, but unconnected, is a modern two-story hall. From a real estate agent's perspective, the building is up-market country — the original structure is preserved, and so are the outdated kerosene lamps, now highly polished and decorating the white wooden walls. Even the organ manages to sound as if it were being pumped by foot pedals instead of electricity. In front of the church is rolling countryside from another age; housing developments of the modern era are fifty yards behind.

The church building and its location speak volumes about an identity in the midst of transformation. There is a traditional, older congregation with its roots in the farming community. But that community has been overtaken by suburban development, and some of the new home owners have tried to make their way into this church.

The building seats about 130. The two Sunday services draw about 85 and 120, including children. Both services use contemporary language. There are occasional forays into a more upbeat tempo, but the standard musical fare is solid, unemotional hymnody. It all goes according to the book. The atmosphere is ordered and decent. The priest is clearly in charge but does not dominate proceedings.

The sermon I heard was a thoughtful commentary on the Supreme Court ruling on the case of Sue Rodriguez, a sufferer from ALS who received assisted suicide. The only other notable deviation from the norm, just before the eucharistic prayer, was a sudden exposition of the meaning of community to the large rabble of children who had entered from their Sunday school classes.

Indeed, explaining things seems to be one of the chief attractions of this church and its leadership. Time and again people mentioned the priest's ability to explain baptism, marriage, and the scriptures in down-to-earth terms. Several mid-week opportunities for adult learning are provided to augment the Sunday program. However, many of the adults who are potential participants are reluctant to add more commitments to an already overextended extended schedule. These are the young families who have found the church to be relaxed and welcoming, as well as a place for learning. They have joined the older congregation, a process that has taken ten years and has not been without conflict.

Does the up-market country and very Anglican style speak in different ways but with equal power to both old-timers and newcomers? Do the symbols of a settled condition give the stability that both groups need to make meaning in their lives? On the one hand, all the familiar symbols are there for the old-timers. Their church building and the worship taking place inside it are modernized but not drastically altered from times past. On the other hand, for the newcomers many of the church ornaments might be present as decorator touches in their living rooms and kitchens. There would be a certain identification with the physical symbols present in the building.

Of course, it takes more than physical symbols to create a lasting attachment to a congregation. The young adults who have made this place their spiritual home were attracted and held primarily by the ability of the spiritual leader to make significant connections with their lives. As at church one, apart from the sermon, there is little in the worship to suggest that it has been radically revised to appeal to new Christians. It seems designed to keep the peace with those who have been there longest. However, the agreed compromise is that the newcomers are welcomed into the congregation, bridges are built, and relationships are formed. The feeling of warmth and the testimonies to the sense of community are genuine.

In appearance and pattern of worship, this is a fairly traditional and conservative Anglican church. Its appeal lies in its solidity and preservation of values. But conservatism is not enough in itself. The church's attractive leadership is valued for bringing church teaching into modern day terms and making it relevant to the lives of new Christians. Furthermore, the priest does not dominate the life of the congregation, although he clearly provides strong direction. A relaxed and non-hierarchical style of community and leadership seems to be the norm.

One of the most significant features of this church is its size. The two congregations are small enough that, within each, everyone can more or less know everyone else and feel they have a personal relationship with the priest. In this context the priest is a pastor and teacher to his flock. The feeling of belonging that the newcomers experience depends upon his ability to make strong personal connections, and these will necessarily be few in number. When people talk about belonging to this congregation they mean, first of all, feeling they have the attention of the priest at a significant point in their lives. Then they move towards being integrated into one of the two small congregations where names and lives are shared. The congregation devotes its attention not so much to program activities as to social events for everyone. The teaching ministry of the priest, particularly around marriage, baptism, and community life, functions as a rite of entry into the congregation.

Church three: a liminal community

The church building is on the main street of the old section of town, now surrounded by burgeoning suburbs. The building, dating from 1840, is built like a shoe box, with a small chancel stuck on the east end. It seats about 200.

When I attended, the building was about three-quarters full. Music began a few minutes before the advertised service time, led by a keyboard, guitars, and a choir. Lyrics were projected onto a wall. Modern, mostly upbeat, hymns were played one after the other until the rector emerged on the scene.

We were welcomed. Newcomers were promised that no one would be embarrassed by anything that would happen. We were assured that we would have an experience of God, and that Jesus would be present amongst us. We were then invited to greet those around us.

The service followed a format loosely based on the modern Anglican rite, although this was only evident to someone familiar with Anglican liturgy because no books were used until we were invited to join in a confession. At this point it became clear for the first time that the service might be a eucharist. The blessing of bread and wine was done facing the congregation from the chancel steps, and everyone present was encouraged to receive communion.

A number of lively commercials punctuated the service, advertising various parish programs. After the service a joint coffee hour was held with those who came early to the next service.

There were some notable features that indicated clearly the intention of this congregation to be a place for young adults to explore the meaning of Christian faith for their lives:

- The emphasis throughout the service was on welcome, belonging, and participation. We are all on a faith journey, and we can expect to be at different stages. No one stage is better than another. This was a service designed for seekers, not finders.

- The music was energetic and engaged people in singing. It was well led, but not oriented to performance.

- The rector was an obvious focus of energy throughout the service, although there were others who read lessons and led the prayers. The sermon was delivered from the aisle without notes. In the middle of the sermon there was a short, amusing, and effective dramatic presentation on the topic.

- The service was geared for young adults — music, leadership, language, issues. Children left for their programs early on.

- There was a strong educational infrastructure. Inquirers could discover the process of belonging through three classes conducted by the rector. There were twelve life groups, led by laypeople, that meet once a week for Christian growth. Other events and programs signalled the church's commitment to the twin pillars of corporate standards and personal development.

This is clearly a church that appeals to people at a transitional point in their lives. Its message constantly emphasizes the validity of the religious quest, the journey rather than the destination, the worth of the seeker, and God as a sympathetic guide rather than a stern judge.

This sense of transition was being put to the test in a dramatic way, because the congregation was being asked to move out of their beloved shoe box into a new building. The argument for moving was based on the potential for continuous growth, the congregational size having levelled off at about 390. However, the present inadequate facilities had a strong emotional pull for even the newcomers. Many liked the fact that the building looked like a church and was different from the other buildings of their suburban landscape. They feared that the corporate energy would be sucked up by a building program, and directed away from the experiential religion they valued.

This church has obviously undergone massive change. An event was announced to honour longstanding members of the congregation. This indicated the intentional managing of what must be a considerable conflict between venerable parish traditions and radical new directions.

Church four: managing the generational gap

This church presents itself on first impression as a very traditional Anglican church. It is situated on a main thoroughfare in the heart of an older residential district. The building is large and old. Inside there is much stained glass and solid oak. The only concession to modernity is the placement of a small altar at the top of the chancel steps, between the choir stalls. The signs announcing what the church has to offer don't suggest anything very radical; however, there is a large, colourful sign for a nursery and daycare, indicating that children inhabit the neighbourhood.

Indeed, this is apparently the case. "The schools are bursting at the seams" and "There's a lot of young families, all with mortgages" were typical comments made by young parents.

The neighbourhood demographics are evident in the congregation that gathers in the pews. Many are older adults, some tracing their membership in the church back to baptism as infants. The next largest group is at least a generation younger, and they bring their small children with them even though a Sunday school program and nursery are available. Mothers rather than fathers seem to dominate this group. At a luncheon, the young women are self-confident and have many social or kinship ties going back to neighbourhood friendships or shared university experiences. Ninety-five per cent of the congregation are Anglo-Saxon.

Reflecting on the three generations of his family sitting side by side, one member said, "It is a strength, but it also makes change difficult."

Why did the newcomers (mostly young families) make this place their church home? "It's close — in the neighbourhood." "We both went to Queen's [University]." "I've been here all my life, and we met through the school." "I have been looking for a church, and when I saw him [the rector] taking his kids to school every day, that did it for me."

In keeping with this network of friendships, kinship, and social identification, the church is low-key about how newcomers belong. There is baptismal preparation and an enquirer's class, but these programs do not seem to be central in the faith expressions of the young women.

Is transition into the church easy? Does the younger generation readily accept the values and norms established by the old-timers? A thoughtful old-timer on the stewardship committee observed, "We can't get them out to meetings. Younger people are more spiritual; it's the older ones who are more materialistic in their values." If this comment is indicative of a wider gulf, then how do the two generations coexist?

The answer lies in the figure of the rector and the message he symbolically communicates in the course of the liturgy.

At first glance there is the promise of an up-to-date liturgy in the enthusiastic bulletin with its upbeat motto about roots and wings. However, any flights are quickly grounded by the dispiriting music through which we enter a time warp of thirty years that continues for the remainder of the service.

In the midst of this unpromising setting the rector emerges as a commanding figure of personal authenticity. Only when he holds centre stage is there energy in the service. His message is clear — "God is your friend" — and this is conveyed in the leaflet, the sermon, and his presence. There is humour and relaxation in his manner: we are invited to laugh at human foibles, parts of the service, parts of the church. The sermon is impressive: clear, thoughtful, well illustrated, convincing, and delivered without notes or hesitation.

However, the rector is also slightly anarchic, making fun of the same church trappings he has adopted. His references to children make it clear that the mischievous child still lives in him. He is a sort of lord of misrule, carrying with him a subterranean threat to overthrow the old, irrelevant order. At the same time he exhibits all the personal authenticity necessary for a leader of a new community, and he invites young people to identify with him. He seems to promise that the old structure will be gently mocked and the new values of community and power sharing will be affirmed and developed.

The priest of this church manages simultaneously two quite distinct symbol systems, the one appealing to the older generation and the other to the young families. This is not to say that everyone over sixty prefers a traditional service with performance-oriented music, and that everyone under forty looks for a charismatic leader oriented to their concerns. What is obvious at this church is the coexistence of two remarkably different emphases, one of traditional structure and the other of a new community. Without self-deprecating humour these two elements would be in continual conflict, both within the rector and in the congregation.

How far can this model go to bring newcomers into the church fellowship and to develop faith, especially among young adults? The symbolic leadership of the rector gives a religious focus to the ties of friendship and kinship that bring in newcomers. However, the current accommodation of the two symbol systems cannot last forever, and the old structures will not serve the new generation. Will this congregation be able to find common, meaningful symbols through which God's Spirit is communicated?

What can we learn?

These four churches share one common feature. They are old. They have old buildings. They have been in existence for more than a human life span. They have congregations that include people who have been around the church for a long time, and who carry with them memories and traditions. However, these churches are also attracting younger adults, and there is some intentionality in their doing so. Like the young adults, the churches themselves are standing on thresholds.

Validating the spiritual quest

Very likely the major force of attraction comes from the spiritual quest of the young adults themselves, a quest that is often founded on a significant event in their lives. In one way or another the significant event was profoundly transforming. Old certainties were swept away. Questions were raised. The effects were often overwhelming and shattering. Even though these events were almost always events of daily life, the language used to describe them had strong religious overtones. Even as the young adults struggled with religious imagery to describe the meaning of these events for their lives, so they often sought spiritual communities as places where these experiences could be valued and given shape and meaning. It is the ability of a church to connect with this quest that attracts young people.

Rites of passage

The most obvious interface between the spiritual quest and the churches are the traditional rites of passage: baptism, marriage, and funeral. The people from outside the church who seek these rites have often been despised by church leaders as simply wanting the formal rituals without any of the commitment that they signify. We need to rethink this attitude. I wonder how many people today want to use the church for empty rituals. The situation is surely that people outside church membership don't want the rituals of the church at all. The traditional rites of the church aren't connecting with people's experience of transition.

The interviews reveal that there is a deep and diverse level of personal liminal experience attached to these rites of passage. People aren't simply coming for baptisms, weddings, and funerals; they are coming to make sense of profound changes in their lives. The woman who tried many churches and found them wanting wouldn't have her children baptized until she found a church that felt like a community to her. Part of her spiritual journey was the difficult disruption of moving from a tightly knit northern community to the vast urban impersonal sprawl of the south. Baptism became a symbol of her search for community and belonging. From experiences like hers we can learn that these rites of passage function somewhat like velcro, attracting and attaching an immense diversity of emotion and longing. We have put a lot of emphasis on explaining the meaning of the rites. How much attention have we paid to understanding the experiences that people bring to them?

This is not to say that explaining the rites is not important. But we would do well to explore in more depth their anthropological dimension and to understand their capacity for expressing and giving shape to the bewildering experiences of transition and change that people bring to them. We need to be aware that they no longer operate in a context in which they are understood: that is one of the reasons they are not sought out as frequently as they used to be. There is an opportunity to redeem these rites and make them available and accessible to people who are trying to make sense of their experiences. The way this happens is through opening up the meaning of the rite with sensitive and clear interpretation, and through offering opportunities for people to reflect on the experiences that brought them to seek the rite, and on how they are reinterpreting these experiences.

Living with nature

We need to take seriously the strong connection that people make between spirituality and nature. In the second research project we used photographs to initiate the conversations, and invariably people chose images from nature to talk of spirituality. Even without the photographs in front of them, when asked to think of images tht expressed their relationship with God, these people all seemed to leap imaginatively into Algonquin Park. There are certainly prophets within the church who have alerted us to natural theology, creation spirituality, and the resources within our tradition that speak to this longing for finding God within the experience of the natural world, but this emphasis doesn't come easily. Here we have another impetus to find and develop the resources of our tradition that will make meaningful connections with the spiritual search of urban seekers longing for experiences of wilderness.

Community and leadership

Finding a church community was very important to all the people I interviewed. However, "community" is a slippery term, carrying with it many associations. Community takes on a more specific meaning when it is seen in the context of profound change and transition. People who are in a liminal state will often seek more intense experiences of community and want attachments with others that have the quality of I-Thou relationships. We saw this in the group of expatriate young adults who shared much of their social life in the church context, and in the church that organized small groups to explore faith in greater depth.

Expressions of community have always been part of the church's life. Intense community often develops in choirs whose members meet regularly and who collectively carry the emotional life of the congregation through their musical leadership. Young parents who gather to organize children's programs often develop strong community bonds. However, in these churches that were attracting young adults we find another dimension of community. They made opportunity for strong relationships to form around the search for meaning. I believe that this type of community will become increasingly important in the life of the church.

We know that leadership plays a vital role in communities. Leaders are not valued for their role so much as for their authenticity. They have to be seen as "one of us," going through the same experiences, wrestling with the same issues, facing the same terrors, celebrating the same joys, drawing on the same resources as the rest of us, yet with a spiritual power that comes from a transparent relationship with God. Interestingly, in all four churches the clergy leaders were very strong teachers, able to make connections between their Christian faith and the life experiences brought by the new Christians. The churches all provided opportunities for adult learning outside the sermon, whether through individual conversation or organized groups.

We can see the importance of teaching and learning in forming church identity. People spoke of the beliefs and values of the congregation when asked what role the congregation had played in their faith development. Teaching expressed in values is wisdom; it is holistic rather than technical.

One of the chief differences among the churches was their size. Smaller churches are able to establish pastoral relationships between clergy and newcomers, and when people are on a spiritual search the demands of these relationships can be quite intense. In larger churches there is the need for more organization to build and maintain intense, interpersonal groups within a more complex structure.

Inviting others

The witness of these new Christians on the subject of inviting others to join the church in which they had found a home is instructive. They were reticent, and their reticence had its roots in a sensitivity to the spiritual quest. Not everyone is on the same search. Some people simply aren't looking. We can learn from this to emphasize respect and sensitivity in our efforts to serve the new people who are attracted to our churches. We shouldn't expect to be attractive to everyone, and we should concentrate on being a welcome place for those who, through whatever circumstances, have been thrown into a search for meaning in their lives.

One church, diverse communities

These churches were all old. This meant that they already had a community of people who formed the congregation. In one way or another the churches were all working at integrating young adults into an existing congregation. These spiritual seekers did not simply join the congregation. With varying degrees of intentionality they formed groups within the congregation. The one constant for all congregations was tension between the established community and the new groups, a tension that is inescapable and necessary for any old church that wishes to be hospitable to new Christians.

There is no one way or right strategy for managing this tension. The four churches were all different, despite the fact that (with the exception of one evening charismatic service) none of them had adopted the strategy of parallel development, by which a whole new congregation is begun in parallel with the old. More important than their unique and varied ways of managing tension was the fact that they created the tension in the first place. They were all convinced that they needed to make a place for spiritual seekers, and they devoted resources to make sure this happened. The dominant culture of our old churches is not intrinsically hospitable to the spiritual quest that animates the lives of many young adults. To create the liminal space within our structured churches where this quest can find a home takes a willingness to risk and considerable courage.

THE DISCOVERY PROJECT

Paul MacLean
Michael Thompson

What We Did

The purpose

In The Discovery Project, a congregation was trying to discover, describe, understand, and interpret the spiritual search of people who didn't do their spiritual searching through the channels of organized religion.

St. Cuthbert's wanted to use this information to see how well the parish was or wasn't responding to the needs, experiences, and gifts of these people. The Discovery Project was the first step in looking for new ways to foster a connection between the church and these people.

The method

We didn't have the resources of Statistics Canada at our disposal. We had to take into account the fact that the people doing the research would be ordinary church folk, not trained demographers. Anyway, we weren't doing the kind of research that could be relied on to draw conclusions about attitudes and values across the country. We weren't trying to establish a control group, test a hypothesis, compare statistically significant numbers, control variables, or be objective at all times. These methods wouldn't have been helpful for exploring the spiritual yearnings of complex human beings in the midst of social interaction.

We were in this primarily for our own learning. Furthermore, we couldn't pretend to be objective. We were all people of faith who belonged to a church, and we were doing this because of our faith. Although our goal was to learn, the research method meant that we would interact with the people we wanted to learn from. Finally, we weren't interested in a ten-year project. We wanted to learn quickly and generalize from a small sample rather than large numbers.

Generating hypotheses, discovering variables, interpreting phenomena, recognizing biases in researchers, using a small sample — these were characteristic of our research, as they are of all qualitative research, a type of research that yields rich information to help us better understand human beings in a social setting.

We decided that the best method for gathering information was the focus group interview, which ordinary folk could conduct with a bit of training and practice. As the time for the interviews approached and anxiety levels began to rise, a member of our team said, "Relax. Don't make it more complicated than it is. We're inviting people to have a conversation." Conducting the interviews in pairs lowered the anxiety level, and it also meant that the two interviewers could compare notes afterwards, picking up different nuances and drawing different conclusions. We were interested not only in what was said, but in how it was said.

We chose the focus group interview as our format because for the interviewees, a group setting was less threatening than a one-on-one interview. And since few people outside organized religion gather in groups to discuss their spiritual yearnings, focus groups seemed the best way for us to achieve our goals.

How the focus groups worked

Participants were recruited by the facilitators/interviewers from among their friends, neighbours, and co-workers and invited to come to a group discussion. Some invited one or more friends who they thought would find the topic interesting to come along.

The result was that everybody in the group knew at least one other group member, and the discussion was able to begin from a basic level of comfort and trust. Although we didn't have difficulty finding people who were willing to join a focus group, the process of inviting people obviously selected those who had interest, courage, and time. We're still reflecting on the higher than anticipated response to the invitation to come to these interviews from the very group of people who don't "come to church."

When the group gathered and the discussion began, members of The Discovery Project worked in pairs, usually with one of the interviewers taking the lead in asking the questions, and the other watching and listening carefully and taking notes. As in the focus group interviews for the Old Churches, New Christians project, the interviewers did not encourage interaction among the participants because we wanted to avoid debate. Since we were asking people to reflect on the values central to their lives, we encouraged respectful listening instead of debate, challenge, and disagreement. The result was a sharing of experience at a fairly deep level, without fear of contradiction or being judged.

To begin the interview, participants were invited to select one visual image from about fifteen, mostly photographs, and use it to talk about spirituality. The visual images provided an excellent and non-threatening way of group building and getting the conversation going. Personal experiences that would have been remote and inaccessible to other group members suddenly became vivid and immediate because they could be attached to an image that was there for all to see. The interest, of course, is in the unique way in which each person sees the image.

The discipline of the interviewers in listening carefully to what people said and in sticking to a time frame of ninety minutes encouraged a similar discipline in the participants, so that a respectful and careful atmosphere was created. As the notes to the interviewers say:

> We are researching and interpreting the living human document. Researchers enter into an "I-Thou" relationship with the participants, based on mutual respect. Our purpose is to discover the meaning of a human experience and to communicate this understanding to others. Rapport and trust are essential to the process. Depth of involvement, not numbers, is the key to quality.

Empowered researchers

The interviewers, a group of ordinary church folk, became immensely interested and took ownership of the project. This would never have happened if the research were in the hands of an outside expert who produced a learned report. Members of the congregation have developed expertise. The information gathered is very much theirs, and they continue to reflect on its meaning.

However, at the outset, some found it difficult to grasp that all this energy was not being expended to recruit members for the church. Then, during and after the interviews, some were frustrated that they had no opportunity to engage the group, express their beliefs and heartfelt commitments, and tell their side of the story. But one of the better descriptions we have heard of the full process of evangelism is, "Go. Listen. Tell." In The Discovery Project we were going to meet people outside the church with the purpose of listening to them. However, we stopped short of telling the Christian version of the spiritual search. Telling has got to be done, but we took the longer view and decided to keep that part of the evangelistic process for another time.

We took a quotation from Martin Buber as our motto and guide to the process. His words were amply fulfilled:

> It is from one person to another that the heavenly bread of self-being is passed.

In search of trustworthy questions

The Discovery Project set out to explore the meaning and practice of spirituality for people with no active church connection. Since the focus groups were essentially an exercise in listening and learning from the church's side, we needed to design a set of questions for outsiders that seemed likely to bring dimensions of their spirituality to the surface. Designing those questions was among the most difficult tasks we encountered.

Our first task was to reach a common understanding of what we mean by "the spiritual dimension" of life. After considerable conversation, we agreed that "spiritual" has to do with the relationship of the inward self to the world in terms of values, meaning, celebration, struggle, and relationships. The word "spiritual" suggests a process of connecting what is within us to what is around us. We needed questions to test our assumption that issues about connecting the inner and outer worlds are real for people beyond the boundaries of church participation. We needed to discover whether there is for them a lively spiritual dimension to life.

We also needed questions that would test our sense that non-church people could have an engaging, lively, and useful conversation about such things without recourse to traditional spiritual language. We needed to know whether or not we could trust our hypotheses:

- that there is a real and lively spiritual dimension to the lives of people who do not participate in church life
- that the difference between participants and non-participants is not a matter of spiritual against non-spiritual people, but of people choosing or not choosing church participation as a means to develop the spiritual dimension of their lives; and
- that non-participants would find stimulating a conversation exploring the spiritual dimension of their lives

Specifically, we hoped we would get at the issue of "spirituality" in three different frameworks.

1. To begin the conversation, a framework that would identify what "spirituality" meant to participants: What do people mean when they say spirituality?

2. A framework in which participants reflected on their lives using categories gleaned from the practices of the church, but described in non-church language: What are people doing that can be understood as spiritual?

3. A more reflective framework in which participants could explore the dimensions of spirituality a bit more theoretically: What are the important elements in spirituality for you,

and how might the church connect more effectively with those elements?

What do people mean when they say spirituality?

The first part of the conversation was open-ended, using pictures to start the reflection and conversation. We chose this way to begin the conversation for a number of reasons. It is often easier to move from the concrete to the abstract than to begin with the abstract. Furthermore, the use of pictures created a common ground of shared experience at the beginning of the time together. Pictures can suggest a variety of meanings, and the interpretation of the pictures began a process of self-disclosure that could be managed by the participants themselves. The diversity of choice and interpretation established that different choices and diversity in interpreting meaning were valid and welcome in the conversation. The pictures were "objective," but they initiated a process of subjective reflection and sharing that was necessary for the process to be both functional and pleasant for participants.

Participants were invited to look at a set of pictures laid out on a table, and to respond to this invitation:

> Think of the word "spirituality," positive or negative. Now choose one of these pictures that conveys to you something of what you mean by "spirituality."

The pictures we used were from the World Council of Churches' collection, *Images of Life*, a collection of images from nature, human struggle and achievement, and human relationships.

What are people doing that can be understood as spiritual?

Our reading, reflection, and consultation yielded a list of areas of human activity in which we understood that a spiritual dimension is present:

- people holding and exploring values, both celebrating the things that matter to them and confronting the dissonance between their values and the values implicit in the life of the world
- people reflecting on meaning and purpose in their lives, and on the impact of their lives on the life of the world;
- people celebrating accomplishments
- people reflecting on and addressing unresolved issues in their lives
- people participating in a community of meaning with others outside their families

While this is undoubtedly an incomplete list, it was good enough because it would allow us to test our assumption that outcroppings of the spiritual dimension of life are present among those who don't participate in churches. The list would also allow us to evaluate our expectation that people who are not members of churches would be able to sustain a lively and meaningful conversation about the spiritual dimension.

Next we had to develop questions that would engage the participants in a discussion of spirituality in their own lives. The questions had to seem important to them and, while emerging out of our own presuppositions and ways of seeing, had to provide a trustworthy and stimulating basis for the participants to explore their own experiences and perceptions about important aspects of being human.

Finally, after several meetings and conversations with others involved in researching spirituality, we developed one or two questions for each area of human activity where the spiritual dimension is present. The questions were designed to engage participants at some depth, and bring to the surface experiences, reflections, and perceptions that would help us to understand and appreciate the spiritual dimension of their lives:

People holding and exploring values, both celebrating the things that matter to them and confronting the dissonance between their values and the values implicit in the life of the world.
1. Take a moment and list all the things you value in your life. (pause) Now choose the two you couldn't live without.
2. Do you think these values are affirmed or denied in our society? Where do you find support for them?

People reflecting on meaning and purpose in their lives, and on the impact of their lives on the life of the world.
1. We will all be remembered, however briefly, when our lives are over. What would you like to be remembered for? What difference do you want your life to make in this world?
2. Who do you want to remember you?

People celebrating accomplishments.
1. What is an accomplishment in your recent life that you took a great deal of satisfaction from? How did you celebrate that accomplishment? (or, How did you express this satisfaction?)

People reflecting on and addressing unresolved issues in their lives.
1. What is an issue or concern that you really haven't resolved yet?
2. What more do you think you need in order to resolve it?

People participating in a community of meaning with others outside their families.
1. Apart from your immediate family, who are the people who are most important to you? What do you get from them?

What are the important elements in spirituality for you, and how might the church connect more effectively with those elements?

The third part of the conversation was more abstract and conceptual.

In the first question, we were looking for insight into people's ideas about the church, and for their interest in something being different in church.
1. If you were on the board of St. Cuthbert's and were discussing how best this church could make a significant difference to the lives of people like you, what would be your one recommendation?

In the last two questions, we wanted to understand participants' conceptual views of spirituality, including what helps or hinders spiritual growth. In addition, we wanted to know what language people with no active church connection use to speak of spirituality.

2. What in your view is most necessary or important for the health and development of the human spirit?
3. What hinders or destroys this development? What helps it? How much control do you think you have over your own development?

Concluding evaluation

From an initial, open-ended exercise using visual images, the questions move successively through the areas of values and society, meaning and purpose, accomplishment and celebration, unresolved issues, and community. The conversation continued with more conceptual questions about the church and the human spirit.

The evening concluded with a brief, informal evaluation:

> We would like to take the last five minutes to give you an opportunity to evaluate our time together. Do you have any comments on how you felt about our discussion?

Beginning with images, focusing on experience, inviting reflection, we hoped to tap into a deep vein of thoughts, feelings, and stories. Would the process engage the participants' energy and interest? Would it help us understand the spiritual dimension of their lives? As we set out, we couldn't know.

What We Learned: Discovering Rich Patterns of Meaning

Strangers become friends: a community of discourse

The thirty-five people who gathered in six focus groups shared only two things. None of them was actively involved in a church. And each of them was willing to give an evening of their time for a conversation about spirituality. Ranging in age from early thirties to early seventies, the largest cluster were aged thirty-five to fifty. Only a few of them had ever met before.

The first remarkable thing about the participants was the eagerness with which they embraced the questions, responded with depth, and connected with one another. Many participants, and all of the twelve facilitators, commented on the quick transition the groups made from breaking the ice to going deep. Participants warmed quickly to the prospect of exploring important questions and issues, shared significant and sometimes difficult stories from their own lives, and provided empathy, support, and encouragement to one another. One participant, who had been particularly critical of the formality and hypocrisy fostered by institutional religion, said at the end of two hours:

> This is just the kind of thing that I've been saying was missing from churches.

Another participant saw the opportunity to deepen and extend the conversation:

> Might there be other questions that would elicit other thoughts, thoughts about something rather different? Is there something about spirituality that escapes us?

One facilitator commented on his surprise at "the very real need and desire that people expressed in relation to the spiritual focus of our discussion."

In many cases, participants formed strong, albeit temporary, bonds. For example, participants responded with empathy to one person's sense that his worth was undermined by bouts of unemployment and underemployment. Respectful listening, encouraged by ground rules that discouraged argument, prevailed as a norm.

In two of the groups, the facilitators had difficulty drawing the conversation to a close at the end of two hours, the outside limit agreed-to at the beginning of the focus group. The conversation was clearly a welcome event for almost all the participants. The structure of the time together, the questions, participants' enthusiastic responses, and the sense of connection that emerged in the groups bore witness to the value of the evening for participants. Clearly, a group of strangers can, in the right circumstances, engage in "spirited" reflection on important questions with a sense of care for one another.

That in itself is an important finding of The Discovery Project. Among thirty-five strangers, there was a rich and vibrant capacity to explore the spiritual dimension of life. At least for these thirty-five, any labelling of people who have no active church connection as "unspiritual" rings hollow.

Understanding what the participants said

Unwrapping the gifts

My cousin David was closest in age to me in the extended family that gathered each Christmas at my grandmother's home. And so it was David and I who exchanged gifts. Reflecting my parents' plain, steadfast approach to things, my gifts to him were often of the obviously useful or traditionally playful kind — a scarf and mitts, or a red fire engine. For his part, David excelled in the giving of exotic gifts. I remember on one occasion unwrapping his gift and not having any idea at all what it was. Part of the pleasure of being the cousin nearest in age to David was anticipating the surprising nature of the gift, and sometimes, spending time after the fact trying to decide what the gift actually was.

The gifts given to the church by the participants in The Discovery Project focus groups are in some ways like David's gifts. We anticipated surprises, and we spent time after the fact figuring out what exactly they were. It takes some time to see as gifts the insights of people who described themselves as "church-wary," of people who have chosen not to (or not chosen to — which amounts to the same thing) participate in the shared life of churches.

But gifts they were: mostly simple gifts, occasionally exotic, and sometimes difficult to understand. The participants shared with us the gift of their own experiences, perceptions, feelings, and points of view. They dug deep for the truth about their lives, and shared generously the truths that they discovered.

Groping for a framework

For us, the researchers, our understanding of spirituality has been changing as we contemplate the stories we heard in The

Discovery Project. It has required letting go of old preconceptions and trusting that something new will make itself available for our understanding, learning, and growth.

In particular, we have been developing a framework for understanding and making sense of the stories, perceptions, reflections and self-disclosure of participants. We believe that this framework offers some clues to the churches on how they might foster a new kind of relationship with those who have said "no" or "we'll see" to the invitation to participate in the church.

Fallibility and wonder:
a framework for understanding spirituality

Social psychologist Robert Kegan, in his book *In Over Our Heads*, describes a radical shift in structures of meaning that has profoundly affected Western society. In the past, meaning was mediated by social systems of meaning. Church, school, legislature, and courts were the formal structures of meaning, and villages, families, towns, guilds, and neighbourhoods were the less formal mediators of meaning. In answer to the question "How am I doing?", there was a more-or-less comprehensive social system of meaning that could provide the answer.

The demise of these social systems of meaning, which began in the nineteenth century, has accelerated over the past fifty years. Social structures are no longer comprehensive, and they have lost the allegiance they once generally held. As a result, mediating meaning, answering the question, "How am I doing?" has become an individual responsibility.

This change has posed a massive challenge for the churches and for other organizations whose stock-in-trade is meaning, as well as for those whom we set out to serve. That challenge showed up clearly in the conversations of The Discovery Project.

Participants described themselves as "church-wary." While spirituality was important to them, they almost universally rejected its institutional forms, rituals, and demands. And their rejection was not just practical — a matter of organized religion's low priority on the scale — but theoretical. Most participants could see no useful connection between their individual search for meaning and the shared framework of meaning that religion represents. "I don't need to belong to somebody else's church with somebody else's rules," said one participant. Another, who had "dropped out" of church participation, said, "The church is supposed to be a vehicle for spirituality and it ends up being a support for an institution." Among the things that people rejected were practices deeply rooted in the values of those who do participate in and lead churches, such as ritual, readings from scripture, traditional theologies of sin and atonement, and most church music. The comprehensive nature of participants' resistance to institutional religion was significant. It wasn't one thing that they disliked, but almost everything we do, from sitting in rows to singing hymns.

Notable for its absence, however, was the optimistic sense that the spiritual dimensions of life were progressing well for participants. The shedding of institutionally mediated frameworks of meaning did not, for many participants, give way to an individualized path in which they had confidence. "I'm not sure I'm living the life that's best for me," was one participant's comment.

Participants also identified the shadow side of freedom from social frameworks. When describing their personal values, there was a widely shared perception that those values were not affirmed by society. "Money takes precedence over love." To cope with the stress of this lack of affirmation for personal values, said one participant, "we need to get back to basic human values."

A sense of uncertainty and fallibility informed much of the conversation in The Discovery Project groups. On the other hand, celebration and wonder also played a role in participants' lives, and in their conversations. Much of the sense of wonder was situated in participants' relationship with the natural world. In fact, one participant went so far as to say, in response to the images used at the beginning of the conversation, "Nature is spiritual. People aren't." But others identified spirituality in terms of diversity, unity, joy, the bonding of generations, and passion.

When asked specifically about accomplishments, most participants identified either the acquiring of new knowledge or skills, or the use of knowledge or skill to resolve difficult and even dangerous situations. In reflecting later on how a church might more effectively connect with people, one participant continued this theme of accomplishment: "It would be better to provide an environment where people can be their best, do their best, and feel rewarded, supported, and accepted."

Notable for its absence was any mention of a public accomplishment or a public celebration. Not a single convocation, baptism, or public outreach project was mentioned. Celebrations were carried out in the presence of family or friends, in an informal, private setting. Intriguingly, goals for future accomplishments included action on ecological concerns, animal advocacy, and advocating and acting for economic development for First Nations people. In every case, these were ideals for the future, not past or present engagements.

On one hand, then, a pattern of uncertainty and fallibility coloured participants' sense of themselves in the world. The question "How am I doing?" was answered, on many occasions, with "I'm not sure," or "Not too well." On the other hand, participants explored their sense of wonder and celebration.

Wonder was often related to the natural world, while celebration was focused on learning and growth, and effective action in challenging or difficult circumstances.

The content of spirituality: conversations and themes

If the interaction between uncertainty and fallibility on one hand, and wonder and celebration on the other, provides a framework for probing the spiritual dimension of participants' lives, what is the content of that dimension? In the conversations of The Discovery Project, a number of themes emerged: identity; vocation; generativity; life competence; insight/understanding; and community/belonging. In each of these areas, at least some participants expressed a passionate engagement.

1. Identity

The question "Who am I?" emerged in the conversations in a number of ways. In one case, it appeared in the guise of taking up sky-diving as a way of dealing with mid-life crisis. While the person did not say, "I am somebody who is strong, adventurous, and unafraid," he might as well have. Another participant described a return to her childhood home as "both an inward and an outward journey. If I want to know who I am, I needed to explore where I came from." Participants acknowledged identity as a cornerstone of the spiritual dimension to life. Said one, "It's important to take five or ten minutes each day for yourself to regenerate and find out what makes you tick."

Another participant explored the difficult relationship between earning power and self-worth. Going through alternating periods of unemployment and underemployment, he said, "made me question who I am and whether I matter." This dimension of self-worth seemed to be an important component in his identity, and other participants in the group acknowledged similar periods and doubts in their own lives.

2. Vocation

The participant who wondered if "I'm living the life that's best for me" shared with many others the need for a vocation to work out an inner passion or drive. The belief that one's life should make a difference was widely held, even in cases where it wasn't clear what that difference was and how to go about making it. The future goals that people mentioned also point to the importance of "call," and specifically the call to share in developing what one participant called "a more humane, livable world." Participants spoke of "making the world a better place," "making the world a lovelier place," and "making a difference in other people's lives."

The need for a life following a vocation and lived with passion emerged as an affirmation of passionate personal engagement with the challenges and beauties of life. But it also emerged as a critical reflection on the absence of passion and the absence of encouragement for people's passionate living in the life of the institutional church. Participants also described a wider social environment that makes passion risky. While they spoke with animation about "living life to the fullest," "living life with passion," and "not being mediocre," they also reflected a widespread lack of encouragement for passionate living. "People think you are strange if you are passionate about your job." "You have to be very careful not to reveal any passions, so that nothing can be held against you." At the same time, "if you don't verbalize passions, after a while they're gone." Vocation — living life passionately from some centre of vitality within — was highly valued by participants, who experienced little external support for passion.

One of the obstacles to passion in church life has to do with participation. Participants showed considerable reluctance simply to go along with the existing practices and rituals of the church. Their desire to make a difference, so vital to their sense of identity and vocation, was given little opportunity to flourish in the church, where things are laid-on, beliefs seem prescribed, and common prayer is scripted. The insight of a friend, who recently spent time in Florence, helped me to understand the power of this issue. "There are no longer any artists in Florence," she said. "They have been told in every way that the great art has already been done by Michelangelo. There's lots of art being done other places, but none in Florence." Echoes of the plight of the churches: "There's lots of spirituality in people's lives; they're just not pursuing it in churches." They've been told in every way that spirituality has already been done.

3. Generativity

A key issue for many participants was the process of passing along values, convictions, and wisdom to the next generation. Parents spoke with energy about their sense of responsibility to help form the values of their children. In some cases, this responsibility to generate a world of opportunity and meaning for growing children was focused and specific. One parent spoke at length of supporting and encouraging her child in befriending a left-out and picked-on child in school. Another spoke of the tension between encouraging a sense of the trustworthiness of most people and a sense of caution in light of the fact that some people can't be trusted. Street-proofing and building trusting relationships were in tension, and she was working hard to resolve it.

One parent talked about intentionally including non-family adults in her children's life, so that they would have healthy examples and ideas from adults who weren't their parents. One older participant spoke with a great deal of affection about the time he spent with his grandson, sharing insights in the course of shared activities.

At the same time, parents grieved over the incongruency between the values they were trying to instill in their children and the values of the society that surrounded them. In one group, participants agreed that the responsibility for sharing values, convictions, and wisdom with children was, for the most part, the responsibility of mothers, not because fathers weren't interested, but because they often didn't have the time. Mothers, they agreed, had to find or make the time. As a result, responsibility for generative activity, for the moral and spiritual formation of children, was in competition with other claims on their time, notably those associated with their workplace. The tension between social values and the moral and spiritual formation of children isn't just a matter of conflict between parents and the society around them, but of conflict within parents' lives.

4. Life competence

Generativity is one element in a more comprehensive set of issues. Life competence issues have to do with "managing" and "performing" in the essential areas of human living. In the conversations of The Discovery Project, life competence was often accompanied by the idea of "juggling" or "tension." Participants described a life in which they felt "too busy" to attend effectively to the essential tasks of adulthood — workplace performance and relationships and family responsibilities being the foremost examples they used.

The integration of family and vocation or career emerged as a common issue in many of the conversations. In this area, one participant disclosed the changing demands of adulthood over time. She felt that she had come to a good balance "for the time being," but added, "I wonder how what I'm doing now will affect what I do later, and how my life will change when family responsibilities diminish?" Adult life competence, then, is not only a matter of functioning effectively in the present, but of laying a foundation in the present for an unknown future.

5. Insight/understanding

By their involvement in the conversations of The Discovery Project, participants disclosed the importance to them of insight and understanding. More in the process of probing, listening, and sharing their reflections, than in the particular reflections that they offered, they identified themselves as seekers after understanding. While *CTV News* may claim the role of "making your world make sense," these participants seemed actively engaged in that task for themselves.

Insight and understanding emerged as an important aspect of each of the other dimensions of spirituality. They had sought and were seeking understanding about their identity, their vocational responsibilities, and the tasks of generativity and other life competence concerns. Their energy for the conversations, and their full participation in them, are evidence of a lively engagement with life around them and life within them.

At the same time, they were largely unresponsive to the church's framework of understanding, and thought it unlikely that church, in its current form at least, could provide resources and support for them in their search to understand themselves and the world. The church, as a mediator of meaning, and as a community in which understanding and insight could grow, was a matter of almost total indifference to many of the participants. A number of participants identified the church with judgemental morality, rather than as a place where people could grow in understanding. While affirming a core conviction in the mission of the church — fostering learning and growth — they rejected the structure, style, and prevailing format in which we embody (or fail to embody) that conviction.

6. Community/belonging

The conversations of The Discovery Project surfaced a great number of sometimes contradictory insights into the issues of belonging and community. Participants described the primary community of family and close friends as important and highly valued. There was no reference to belonging to a group with a shared purpose, although, as we noticed earlier, some participants had an ideal of belonging to such a group in the future.

In only one of the groups was there any enthusiasm for a secondary community with wider membership than the association of family and close friends. That group conceived of such a secondary community as a place to explore and learn, and to receive support in areas of living that were difficult to manage with the limited spiritual and emotional resources of a nuclear family.

Community, in this case, is a place where deep concerns are addressed. Even in the group that was enthusiastic about a secondary community, that enthusiasm was driven by the hope for a place to deal with important or difficult life issues, to draw upon the resources of others, and to share resources with them. By and large, the primary community of family and friends was adequate to participants' need to belong; a secondary community would serve a different need. A secondary community was not, for these people, an end in itself, but a means to other ends, a resourceful environment in which to work at the issues and dimensions of life identified above.

Yes to Spirit, no to church

The conversations of The Discovery Project disclose dimensions of participants' lived experience and reflection that suggest, quite compellingly, the rich significance of spirituality in their lives. Beginning with the tension between uncertainty and fallibility on one hand, and wonder and celebration on the other, these dimensions are contained squarely within the domain of human experience that has characteristically been served by organized religions.

Participants in the conversations of The Discovery Project were, for the most part, sensitive to and concerned about issues that the churches would identify as core spiritual issues. Furthermore, they were, to a significant extent, aware of the limitations that hindered their capacity to address the spiritual dimension and issues of their lives. Why is it that they do not see participation in church life as a place to address those issues?

Lack of time for spirituality

There are some relatively easy answers, however partial. First, they identified lack of time as a significant limitation on their activities. Given the many demands of home and workplace, participants were under significant time pressure. Recently, St. Cuthbert's hired a student to contact parishioners who had stopped participating in the parish's life. We wanted to understand why they had dropped out, and whether there was anything in our common life that had made their experience negative. With a couple of exceptions, there wasn't anything negative. Quite simply, other priorities were taking up their time.

Lack of interest in spirituality

A second relatively easy response is that they don't care enough about spiritual issues. Sometimes church members and leaders compare the amount of time people spend on other pursuits with the amount they spend on spiritual matters and come to the conclusion that spiritual issues just aren't very important to people. In fact, there is some truth to this view. The Old Churches, New Christians project considered people who have reconnected with church. For all of them, there was a precipitating critical event, sometimes in the past, sometimes in the present, that intensified their engagement with life's spiritual dimension enough for them to move towards involvement with organized religion. Clearly then, for some people in some circumstances, spiritual concerns need to reach a critical stage before they take steps to address them, or make new choices about priorities for their use of limited time and energy.

The church discourages seekers

A third response blames the church for its lost (or never found) relationship with people. Critics point to rigid moral authoritarianism, hypocrisy, and self-righteousness as active ways in which the church discourages seekers from entering, and to irrelevance, traditionalism, outmoded beliefs, and inertia as more passive ways.

While these three sets of responses help us to understand why seekers engaged in the spiritual search do not see the church as a place to pursue their searching, the conversations of The Discovery Project invite us to look beyond these simple answers to an exploration of the changing dynamic among individual, world, and church, a changing dynamic that challenges both individuals and churches to understand and act in new ways.

Landmarks: how The Discovery Project has changed one church

The Discovery Project has set us on a new journey at St. Cuthbert's. On one level, not much has changed. Worship is at the same times, the Bible study groups still meet, the choir rehearses, youth group and confirmation continue their rhythms, and women's groups engage in a variety of meetings and activities. But on a deeper level we have learned that we don't have to be something we are not in order to be attractive as a congregation. We can be ourselves, and yet take on new directions in our journey.

That journey has specific landmarks, points of departure, and hopes. We are not a "model church." Our journey and its intended goals reflect our gifts, our character, and our understanding of our environment. Spiritual needs take different forms in different times and places. But we have begun to identify landmarks in our journey.

For example, the most notable area of growth in our parish life is in the number of outreach activities accessible through our church. We have taken seriously the desire of people to make a contribution to the life of the world, and their need for "low-hurdle" points of access and organized, ready-made opportunities to serve others. *A landmark of renewal in historic-cultural churches will be a renewed understanding of outreach ministries that offer structured opportunities to people in their desire to make a difference.*

We have begun to look for specific strategies for effective ministry with people in periods of transition. For example, while our Sunday school was, in theory, for junior kindergarten to grade six, there have been almost no participants from grades five and six for the past several years. Not only were these kids melting away, but also they were taking their families and younger siblings with them. The lens of liminality has helped us to understand that kids aged ten to twelve are crossing a threshold into adolescence. At that threshold, they resist being included in a children's program, and place a high value on belonging. This year, we have identified them as a separate group, and developed a low-content, high-relationship, active group life. While the group has grown from one or two participants each week to ten or more, the real learning for us is that, if we pay attention to thresholds and transitions, we can serve and support people in making those transitions. *A landmark of renewal in the historic-cultural churches will be active attention and focused response to the thresholds and transitions of people's lives.*

We have begun to experiment with an alternative time and style of worship. In responding to the findings of our research, we have opted, initially, not for the "upbeat" soft-rock celebration, but for a short, contemplative gathering following a simple meal on Saturday evenings. Our intention is that each gathering will focus on a theme that discloses the divine-human encounter, with an emphatic commitment to reflecting the human story accurately and recognizably. Our hope is that participants will experience their stories as connected to and informed by the wisdom of the biblical tradition, and begin to experience the community and its story as a source of meaning and encouragement. That hope is rooted in our learning from The Discovery Project, as we search for new ways to invite people into community, and effective ways to help them make contact with the Spirit through story and ritual. At the end of six (monthly) such gatherings, we will evaluate our efforts and plan our next steps. *A specific landmark of renewal in the historic-cultural churches will be a willingness to experiment, and a commitment to evaluation. Especially in the area of worship, new patterns in naming and celebrating the divine-human encounter are not a matter of adopting someone else's strategy, but of developing local strategies and evaluating their effectiveness honestly.*

Implications for People and Parishes

Michael Thompson

Recovering the Mission of the Historic-Cultural Churches

For Christians who are tired of church growth gurus whose prescriptions have failed, and for churches in which a shift to charismatic, conservative evangelical, or mega-church Christianity is either impossible or inconsistent with their heritage and identity, there is good news.

The future of historic-cultural Christianity need not be one of empty churches, dispirited leaders, and failed mission. Our search began as a quest for viable strategies for historic-cultural churches to continue God's work in the world. Both Old Churches, New Christians and The Discovery Project identify a broad base of spiritual seekers whose needs are not addressed by mega-church, conservative evangelical, and charismatic forms. When all the people who are predisposed to these forms of church have been successfully recruited by them, the world will still be home to hundreds of millions of others, people with no active relationship to any community of faith.

Many of these "leftovers" are deeply moved by the spiritual dimension of life. And many of them yearn for community, resources, and encouragement in their seeking. For those who believe that our responsibility is not to plagiarize the story of other churches, but to search out and tell the next chapter of our own story, the "leftovers" are our challenge and our opportunity. In relationship with them we will find the renewal we seek. Who are they? What can we know about them? What intention can form the basis for a healthy and authentic relationship with seekers?

Who are the seekers?

Jesus didn't say, "I am among you as one who recruits." While much of the energy of the gurus focuses on effective recruiting and the building of strong institutions, the Spirit may be asking the historic-cultural churches, "Will you be among 'them' as a community that serves?"

The first important contribution of Old Churches, New Christians and of The Discovery Project is to put a face to "them." "They" are people who express a deep concern for the spiritual dimension of life, but do not find themselves well-served by churches. "They" are people made in God's image and likeness who themselves express a desire to serve, to make a difference by the way they live. "They" are people for whom the dimensions of spiritual searching correspond to the spiritual concern and resources of churches, but many of them have not found meaningful access to that concern and those resources.

In light of all this, the failure of our weak historic-cultural churches to become strong by adopting the program of one church growth guru or another is good news. If we were successful in doing so, we would simply abandon a vast, if difficult, dimension of human spiritual searching: that represented by participants in Old Churches, New Christians and The Discovery Project.

Thresholds: searching for resources at a time of transition

These two projects offer us considerable insight into the spirituality of seekers. In particular, Old Churches, New Christians identifies the preference for communities in which authenticity is valued over role or status, and dynamism over routine. Further, it identifies the tendency of young adults to seek a connection with a faith community as a result of profound personal change. This liminal or threshold state seems to be a very common precursor to seeking active connection with a church, if not an actual prerequisite. The important thresholds identified in Old Churches, New Christians include death, divorce, marriage, birth, and moving to a new community or country. In each of these, there is evidence of considerable inward reflection on the part of those experiencing it, and of an outward search for resources and community as people explore the new way of life ushered in by these transitional events.

The Discovery Project widened the scope of our understanding of transition and search in people's lives. Out of the core question "How am I doing?" emerge the symmetrical needs for a place to celebrate life's wonder, and a place to address personal fallibility and life's brokenness. In more detail, people's searching includes dimensions of identity, vocation, community/belonging, generativity, insight/understanding, and life competence. In light of the findings of The Discovery Project, our conception of threshold experiences is augmented beyond "hatches, matches (and un-matches), and dispatches" to include a more comprehensive list of experiences in which people ask the question, "How am I doing with this?"

These dimensions of spiritual searching invite a response from historic-cultural churches. People exploring transitions and challenges in their lives are often open to, if not actively seeking, a community in which authenticity is valued and rewarded, and in which they can find resources, encouragement, and companionship as they negotiate the changing and challenging patterns of their lives.

Serving: a strategy rooted in God

But the opportunity offered to us is an opportunity for serving, not for recruiting. Recruiting, either to institutions or to belief systems, is not a viable strategy for making contact with the church-wary. In Old Churches, New Christians, those who had reconnected with the church emphasized its resourcefulness in responding to the particular transition in which they found themselves. They did not encounter barriers of belief or of institutional allegiance that they were required to affirm before they were taken seriously and supported. In The Discovery Project, those with no active church connection did not describe their spiritual searching in terms of right belief or of membership in an institution, but in terms of the vital issues of their daily life.

Why do we seek to make contact with those who are not our members? What is the theological framework that sustains us in that contact? Unless we ask and answer these questions, then we will almost certainly engage in the activity of which we are, in many instances, already suspected — subtly recruiting members to support an institution.

At the core of the renewal of historic-cultural churches lie the questions:

- What is our missiology — what "business" are we in?
- What is our ecclesiology — what organizational framework of structures and patterns will support us in being effective?
- What is our theology — what understandings of God undergird the previous two?

Because we are going to be in the business of supporting people in developing spiritual resources and patterns that address the issues of their life in the world, we need to organize our structures, resources, and patterns of activity around that core commitment, and we need a theology that is consistent with that preference. Theologies that focus on the primacy of religious belief, religious experience, or institution-building will undermine our long-term capacity to function as servants.

The God revealed in creation, in the history of Israel, and in Jesus, demonstrates active concern for the well-being of the world and exhibits a consistent effort to engage human beings in actively sharing that concern. In the biblical record, religious belief and experience are often not the heart of the matter, but secondary, though valuable, dimensions of the relationship between God and persons. The God of the Bible can, without contortions, be understood as a God whose mission is in and for the world, and whose primary engagement with human persons is to challenge, encourage, nurture, and equip them to share in that mission.

This biblical God is vitally interested in the quality of our engagement with the likes of the participants in Old Churches, New Christians and The Discovery Project. Participants in our research expressed a consistent desire "to make a difference." Within family, community, and workplace, they lived in tension between their ideals and their limits. They spoke with some longing about a desire to extend their impact beyond their immediate environment, and some hoped that the church might be a community that would facilitate growth in that direction. God created human beings to bless and tend the earth. God called Israel to be an exemplary community founded on justice, hospitality, and compassion. God in Christ served and taught those who were ignored and repudiated by religious institutions and their leaders. God cares deeply about what happens to the human impulse to "make a difference." Activating, nurturing, and celebrating that impulse lies at the heart of the mission of God in creation, in calling Israel, and in Christ.

A new framework for the churches' engagement with people

As the historic-cultural churches leave behind the machinery of Christendom, which provided the rationale for church participation until the middle of this century, we find ourselves looking for new ways to connect with the gifts and spiritual longing of our neighbours. The symbiotic relationship between historic-cultural churches and their host societies has, for the most part, dissolved:

- There is no longer any shared understanding that church participation is a vital element of citizenship.
- The mission field, or what Loren Mead calls the "mission frontier," is no longer at the distant edge of some empire, but local, "at the door of the church." The experience of many clergy and lay leaders, like those in Old Churches, New Christians, is that the mission frontier is inside the church door as well.
- The social apparatus of North America no longer actively supports Christianity. This is not, as some hold, evidence of religious pluralism, but rather an emerging ethos that marginalizes not just Christianity, but any concrete historic embodiment in community of the spiritual dimension of being human.
- Religious institutions and their practices no longer serve as the "location of choice" for people addressing the spiritual dimension of their lives. In the 1991 census, within

the parish boundaries of St. Cuthbert's, the percentage of people claiming "no religious affiliation" overtook the percentage claiming even nominal Anglican affiliation, even though we are located in a narrow north-south corridor identified by a demographer as "the natural turf" of the Anglican Church.

Within our host society, Christianity has moved, in the last half-century, from being vital to being beside the point, from being actively supported to being effectively ignored, from forming part of the society's governing structure to being exiled to the sidelines. But during the long inning of Christendom, the historic-cultural churches have developed a habit of care for our culture's well-being, though admittedly with mixed results. It would not be appropriate or faithful for us to abandon that habit of care, even though it is clearly not possible to exercise it under the terms, now withdrawn, of Christendom.

The situation in which we find ourselves has more in common with the first three centuries of the Christian story than with the intervening seventeen. As we enter the third Christian millennium, we are surrounded by a culture in which organized religious institutions have lost their authority for many of our contemporaries. But like those early centuries, ours is an era of widespread concern with the spiritual dimension of human life. Because we have lost our "implicit" status in the life of our society, we are, like the first Christian communities, able to offer an alternative to its core organizing principles of markets and consumerism. As the largest generation in human history, the baby boomers, grows increasingly dissatisfied with the accumulation of material wealth and temporal power, they will, like the participants in Old Churches, New Christians and The Discovery Project, be probing the spiritual dimension of life with considerable focus and energy. Will we be there to serve them? Will the form in which we offer that service be comprehensible, accessible, even attractive?

Real renewal: the church as servant-teacher

Jesus of Nazareth challenged a tired and cynical religious establishment to open itself to the concrete spiritual needs of those it excluded. He stepped outside the constraints of that establishment and engaged people with imagination and courage, addressing their spiritual needs as a servant-teacher. The pattern of the servant-teacher emerged among the earliest followers of Jesus in the first "order" of ministry to be established — that of the deacon, the servant-teacher. As Christendom, with its sense of power, privilege, and status, became the dominant Western form of ecclesiastical self-consciousness, the order of deacon became marginal, existing until recently in the Anglican and Roman Catholic churches as, for the most part, a transitional order leading to priesthood.

Challenging the marketplace gods

Circumstances may be more decisive than internal theological debate in stimulating the historic-cultural churches to renew the diaconal heart of our vocation. In our time, the truly powerful "religious" establishment may, in fact, be the one that attempts to exploit the deepest human yearnings, identifying them with individual accomplishments in the consumer marketplace. It is the gods of workplace and marketplace who command the absolute loyalty of persons, loyalty that the church once commanded. Where once the church enjoyed the privilege of identifying winners and losers (*extra ecclesiam nulla salus*

— "outside the church there is no salvation"), the power to decide who wins and who loses has devolved to the marketplace. The church may grieve at the loss of one kind of power and, at the same time, discover the possibility of another, more faithful, understanding of power — the power to serve and to teach.

The 1998 Volvo advertisement — "at last, a Volvo that can save your soul" — is a blunt line from the tireless chorus of the marketplace gods. Such an ad reminds us that there are plenty of people ready to exploit the human need for community and spiritual meaning and purpose. Still, we are in no position to complain about the empty posings of market religion if we have made no attempt to follow Jesus in addressing human spiritual need with the spirit of the servant-teacher. The time has come for the historic-cultural churches to retrieve the ministry of the deacon as a way of thinking and acting, a way of seeing ourselves as the church in relationship with the world God loves.

At our best, faith communities in the historic-cultural tradition can inform, deepen, and support people's search for ways of living that reflect the human vocation of covenant or partnership with God. Though our neighbours might not use that language of partnership to describe their search, we can focus our resources, energy, and vision to reflect our own vocation as a servant-teacher community. We need to renew our confidence that our communities' resources can support and encourage human spiritual searching. And we need to renew our strategy for offering our tradition as an alternative to the dehumanizing gods of market consumerism.

We need to cut ourselves free from our entanglement with mega-church, conservative evangelical, and charismatic traditions. For too long, we have understood them as our rivals. They are not. They have developed a capacity to serve the spiritual needs of some — even many — in our society. But there are many others who resist being engulfed by the programmatic reach of the mega-church, the immodest absolute truth claims of the conservative evangelicals, and the imposing norms of religious experience in the charismatic movement. If there are many who respond to these models of church, there are many more who do not.

To the many who are still seeking, the only alternative to the powerful and dehumanizing idolatry of the consumer marketplace is either some slight vestige of church formation or a vague new-age yearning. As historic-cultural churches, our real competition is the cynical reduction of human persons to bit players in the theology of the market. In Old Churches, New Christians, and especially in The Discovery Project, we hear the voices of those whose own experience has begun to unmask the inhumanity of the religion of marketplace consumerism. We encounter those whose deep values are, by their own estimation, unsupported by the society around them. We meet those who ask the question, "How am I doing?" and discover both reasons for celebration and a basis for lament in their answer. Now is not the time for us to cut them adrift, to adopt the alien strategies of mega-church, conservative evangelicals, or charismatics in hopes of ensuring our own survival. Now is the time to engage the seekers, to challenge the hegemony of the consumer marketplace, and to offer a human spiritual alternative to cynicism or despair.

To have glimpsed the pressing need for such engagement on our part, however, is not the same as being equipped to undertake it. It is one thing to reclaim the church's corporate identity as servant-teacher in response to the seeking of our contemporaries. It is another to muster the will, imagination, strategy, and perseverance that will effectively embody that identity.

Strategy for the Servant-Teacher Church

Listening for the question: turning our ears outward

Old Churches, New Christians and The Discovery Project share an outward-facing orientation. One looks at the threshold of church participation, and asks those who have recently crossed it to identify the circumstances in their lives that prepared them to cross. The other explores the lives of those who show no inclination to cross that threshold, and tests the hypothesis that there is a spiritual dimension to their lives. Both projects disclose a ferment in people's lives, a search that people undertake in order to answer the question, "How am I doing?"

The first implication of these projects for churches in the historic-cultural tradition is to teach us to listen for that question and to discern its real content. The threshold events of Old Churches, New Christians, and the focused dimensions of spiritual searching revealed in the conversations of The Discovery Project, would not have been unearthed if we had not begun by listening. Neither would they have been discernible if we had not entered the conversation with some idea of what we were listening for. Because we began by asking thoughtful questions and listening with care to the response, we were entrusted with a framework, however rudimentary, for understanding the spiritual lives of people outside organized religion.

Part 1 of the strategy: "being there" for people at threshold moments in their lives

Old Churches, New Christians discloses that liminal events or turning points in people's lives are a stimulus for spiritual searching. It also discloses the kind of community preferred among those who, at a life-changing threshold, have sought community support and illumination for their journey by stepping into the church. The findings suggest a two-pronged strategy for the servant-teacher church.

The first part of the strategy is the commitment to "being there" — to placing ourselves somehow alongside those who are negotiating life-changing thresholds. In an earlier, perhaps simpler time, the church developed a ritual engagement with three such passages: the birth of a child, forming a life partnership in marriage, and death. Later, a fourth "threshold" celebration emerged in the use of confirmation primarily as a puberty rite at or shortly after the onset of adolescence. These rituals are less sought-after than was once the case. For example, the confirmation class (all twelve to fourteen years of age) at St. Cuthbert's in 1946 had sixty-one members. In 1999 there were seven. All the same, there are still some who look to the church to provide teaching and interpretation in some of life's thresholds.

How effective are we in providing truly helpful resources and support in even these limited circumstances? Do we see our engagement with adolescents preparing for confirmation as an opportunity to serve and support them in the difficult and often-abandoned passage to adulthood? Or do we see this as one last chance to bribe or threaten some young people into institutional compliance?

One place for historic-cultural churches to begin our renewal is in re-examining the approaches we take to thresholds at which people still (though in smaller numbers) seek our support. Are we seeing them as opportunities to recruit, or as instances of the call to be servant-teachers? Especially since our experience suggests that God has not granted us the charism of recruitment, might we finally be willing to take on the charism that *has* been granted, that of serving, interpreting, and illuminating the tumultuous passage of our neighbours across the challenging thresholds of their lives?

Old Churches, New Christians affirms that persons in transition are open to new possibilities for understanding and embodying the spiritual dimension of their lives. As we develop the mind of Christ the servant-teacher in our churches, the thresholds in the lives of those around us create opportunities for us to serve and to teach. Two dimensions of that opportunity suggest themselves.

The first is a renewed attentiveness to transition ministry already embodied in our tradition through infant baptism, confirmation, marriage, and burial.

The second is a recognition of other thresholds, increasingly common in our age. Those who framed our tradition could not have been expected to foresee the mobility of today's society. There is no sacrament of "moving away" or "moving in." We have no framework for recognizing the vocational arabesques by which people move from one job to another, or to unemployment, or from a period of unemployment to new work. There is no ritual recognition of young people leaving their home and community, perhaps forever, to attend university or college or to work in another community or country. These intensely liminal realities were not much a part of life when our traditions were forming in the crucible of the distant past. Today, their ritual recognition, and the development of a teaching and pastoral practice to illuminate and support those who move through them, might do a great deal to re-connect the historic-cultural churches with the spiritual lives of those around us.

As I write, two years after The Discovery Project began, the parents of twenty-one households are gathering at St. Cuthbert's for the first night of an eight-night "Practical Parenting" course. Of those twenty-one households, not one is on our parish list. It has taken over eighteen months to begin responding to what we learned, to find the right point of entry and the right gifts, to connect with our neighbours by serving a need expressed both in The Discovery Project and in a follow-up focus group held six months ago with parents of young children.

Our newly ordained deacon is recruiting a group of people in our parish, among them a young woman little interested in church but very much interested in making a difference, to provide tutoring for children at a ministry centre in a nearby housing development. Our deacon has been working a half-day a week there, both to become aware of ministry outside of a traditional parish setting, and to provide a link between our ministry and theirs.

Recently the chair of the Christian Education Committee approached me, concerned that we haven't developed a way to serve members of our own parish who are in crisis. "There is a lot of hurt in people's lives, but we often don't know what it is until they disappear or come apart." She wants to meet with me and some others to see if there is some way to invite people into a deeper conversation than is usually the norm in our common life. She knows it can help, because she and a number of other women in their sixties and seventies have been meeting regularly to talk about their shared but varied experiences of growing older.

A nearby congregation has discovered that many of the volunteers in their weekly shelter program are not parishioners, but friends and neighbours. Another discovered that their involvement in Habitat for Humanity provided a vehicle for many inactive members and non-members to become involved in making a difference.

A conference on "Spirituality in the Workplace" drew hundreds of people to the University of Toronto campus in the spring of 1998, offering an opportunity for people to make a vital connection between their work and their spirit.

The common thread of these experiences is that they serve a dimension of human spiritual development. While The Discovery Project has been an essential part of how St. Cuthbert's is developing, the servant-teacher model is springing to life in a variety of ways and places. Churches and church leaders are working hard to understand the way our culture has changed and continues to change, and to create opportunities to connect with the spiritual reality of those formed by that changed and changing culture. The Discovery Project is part of a much larger movement, its contribution vital to our congregation, and especially to the developing understanding of the church leaders who shaped it and carried it out. Perhaps the most significant implication of The Discovery Project is that the effect of doing it is probably larger than the effect of reading about it. It gave us an opportunity to explore a common concern with those outside of our institutional culture, to learn from them, and to reflect on our life in light of our learning.

It also contributed to our understanding as we planned it. The effort of finding ways to talk about spirituality without reverting to the coded language of our religious tradition invited us to speak more plainly and think more clearly about our own spirituality. Planning The Discovery Project changed the way we thought and talked about our spiritual lives. The simple act of looking outward has changed us. What we found will change us more, if we can adopt the attitude of servant-teacher.

Part 2 of the strategy: looking inward and renewing the heartbeat of Christian community

None of these initiatives of engagement with our environment demands that we sacrifice the heartbeat of worship and learning within the church. While we attempt to take seriously the needs of those who worship with us, we will still find the biblical story and the sacrificial meal at the centre of worship. Worship will continue to be directed towards the God we encounter in word and sacrament, with Bible, hymns, pews, and "somebody else's rules." Why? Because Somebody Else is precisely the One into whose presence we gather, by whose dream and daring alone we are called to serve and teach. Trading the integrity of worship for the approval of the church-wary is a bad bargain.

Worship

There is, however, a crisis of imagination in the worship patterns of historic-cultural churches, a failure to engage the imagination, experience, and concern of worshippers that renders God and God's promises less real. Herbert Anderson and Robert Foley address this failure in *Mighty Stories, Dangerous Rituals,* asserting that "public worship does not adequately mediate divine presence because it is inattentive to the human story." That human story emerges in the conversations of Old Churches, New Christians and The Discovery Project, and can become our teacher as we address the challenge of renewal in our worship.

Perhaps it is those congregations who acknowledge and embrace their own liminal existence, recognizing that as a congregation they stand on a threshold at a point of transition, who are best able to respond to those standing on thresholds in their own lives. Of the congregations researched in Old Churches, New Christians, the tension between liminality and familiar structures is apparent in three. It is precisely those tensions that need to be addressed in order to engage meaningfully with people for whom liminality is the daily reality. Repentance — which means turning around, changing your mind — is a primary communal task for congregations unwilling or unable to relinquish the stable patterns of the past in favour of a less certain but more promising embrace of liminality. If the experiences that encourage people to seek out spiritual resources are powerful, often shattering encounters with change, uprooting, and loss, the churches whose goal is to sustain their own comfort in familiar and ordered patterns will not be able to serve those seeking God.

We have learned that threshold transitions are the motivating force in the spiritual journey. The creative tension between fallibility and wonder and between struggle and celebration, and the landmark issues of identity, vocation, competence, understanding, generativity, and belonging — these are what drive people in their spiritual searching. As we allow these threshold transitions to illuminate the divine-human encounter in worship, they deepen and focus the human dimension of worship. Having taken seriously the reality of human struggle and celebration, we can point with authority to the God whom we worship, who heals us, strengthens, sustains and forgives us, and sends us into the life of the world as partners in a mission that heals, forgives, strengthens, and sustains.

Learning

The second "heartbeat" activity of the Christian community is gathering to learn. The fact that, in many of our churches, the same five or ten per cent of members turn up for events sponsored by the Christian Education Committee suggests a gap between our teaching ministry and our own members. In response to our invitation to learn, those who worship regularly seem as hesitant to participate as are the church-wary. It is worth considering the possibility that what we have learned from the church-wary might strengthen our own internal ministry of learning and teaching. Might the framework of spirituality gleaned from The Discovery Project be a useful lens for renewal in the way we learn? The identification of "liminal" or threshold experiences can be a clue to the development of effective and life-touching experiences of learning. A central affirmation in theories of adult learning is that adults learn when they have something real at stake. A challenge, a need for new resources or insights to address a new situation, a desire for significant change in their lives — these are the basic catalysts for learning.

We have an opportunity to develop educational initiatives that might serve the church-active and the church-wary alike. In fact, in developing our educational ministry, having the church-wary in mind might help us connect with the learning needs of those who participate in the worship life of our churches but resist or ignore our educational programmes. Those who worship in our churches are no less affected by the thresholds and transitions that so many in our world are struggling to sort out.

Worship and learning, the heart of Christian life in community, can be informed and strengthened by the findings of Old Churches, New Christians and The Discovery Project. It is not only those with "no religious affiliation" who sometimes find our worship uncompelling and disconnected from the stuff of struggle and celebration in their lives. While acknowledging the continuity of ritual and story that has been entrusted to us and that we are called to hand on, not to cast off, we are called to attentive care for the human strands of story that gather in our churches Sunday by Sunday. And, while acknowledging our responsibility to teach the tradition, we are called to find ways to teach that are connected to the search for meaning and purpose in the face of liminality and contingency, a search that will be the primary basis for any learning among many of our contemporaries.

Clarifying the Identity of the Historic-Cultural Churches

Marks of renewal: a provisional framework for historic-cultural churches

Our challenge is to identify common patterns of life that would sustain historic-cultural churches in a shared identity. What are the shared practices, catalogue of virtues, and models of Christian adequacy that will bind us together as the next generations of a tradition rooted deep in history and attentive to our relationship with the culture and society around us?

1. Partnership with God in caring for the world

The first element of a renewed identity for the historic-cultural churches is the retrieval of our confidence in God's mission in and for the world. As our churches perceive it, God's desired outcome is not gaining subscribers to a belief system, to an institution, or to a normative palette of religious experiences. Instead, we conceive of working in partnership with God in caring for the world. This metaphor of partnership with God is an entry-point familiar to both the biblically literate and to those who yearn to define their lives in terms of "making a difference." A theology that empowers us to participate in God's mission can help us begin to make connections between churches and the church-wary.

2. Active and attentive humility in our encounter with the world

The second core element in our renewed identity is active and attentive humility in our encounter with the world. As churches concerned with mobilizing human gifts for partnership with God, we are called to pay attention to the struggles and celebrations of those around us. We need to name and celebrate those occasions when people act for the common good. We need to stand beside those who seek new directions, offering the resources and challenges of our faith and tradition as support and encouragement to them. We need to understand the spirit in the lives of those who are not part of our congregations, and discern the working of the Spirit who gives richly to us that we may give richly to others.

3. Careful and focused intention in the way we order the internal life of our churches

The third element in our renewed identity is a careful and focused intention in the way we order the internal life of our churches. While we cannot discard our heritage — the songs and stories that have brought us this far on the journey — we can continually review the manner in which the songs are sung and the stories told. When we discover that the songs no longer echo in people's lives and the stories no longer connect us to God, we have work to do, not only for the church-wary, but for our own internal life as well. The conversations of Old Churches, New Christians and The Discovery Project can help us understand the spiritual dimensions, not only of the church-wary, but also of the church-weary, who long for an encounter in worship and learning that is lively with the presence of God, and that takes us, and our predicaments, seriously.

4. Assuming the mantle of the servant-teacher

Finally, the renewal of historic-cultural churches depends on our assuming the mantle of the servant-teacher. We must become communities that nurture the human capacity for thoughtfulness, care, and principled living wherever we find it, and that illuminate the spiritual journeys of our neighbours, not because we expect them to join our church, but because we hope to support them in their engagement with the world. For those who look deeper or move closer, we can provide formative and transformative opportunities to learn, and worship to give voice to the song of praise and wonder welling up in their lives, even as we struggle together with life's sharp edges and hard passages.

But not all, and perhaps not many, will join our churches. In Jesus' healing of ten lepers, nine never came back. Was the healing a failure?

A respectful "two-track" strategy honours both past and present

It is not uncommon for congregational leaders to separate the old and the new into segregated worlds. The assumption seems to be that old patterns will eventually die away while new ones emerge. Palliative care for the old and midwifery for the new! While patterns and practices do come to an end and new ones do emerge to take their place, the reality is far more complex than this simple assumption suggests.

At St. Cuthbert's, in the aftermath of The Discovery Project, we are discovering that leadership and energy can transform existing patterns and practices, and root new developments in the wisdom and resources of heritage. For example, the hope of our worship experiment is "that participants will experience their stories as connected to and informed by the wisdom of the biblical tradition, and begin to experience the community and its story as a source of meaning and encouragement." This is the same hope we have for the community that already gathers for a more traditional eucharistic celebration on Sunday mornings. While the developmental track demands that we be clear about the hopes and principles that inform our strategies, those same hopes and principles can strengthen and inform existing practices as well. Energy applied to developing new patterns will enliven the old ones.

Conversely, the very past for whose demise we often so fervently wait provides boundaries and landmarks that can help us avoid dead ends and destructive paths. Over lunch a couple of years ago, a friend suggested that spirituality would be more appealing "if it didn't have all that weird Bible stuff" attached to it. True enough, given the way the Bible has been used as an instrument of social control and metaphysical bullying. But as a richly textured story of how humans have understood and expressed the divine-human encounter, it is a gift from the past. And although it may confound us, the fact that we cannot discard it forces us to return to it, to discover riches that we might otherwise never have encountered.

Then, as soon as we accept this gift from the "old patterns," we hear the voice of the new, resisting some former interpretations, finding new understandings, discovering new dimensions of the divine-human encounter buried in the text. As those meanings surface, they illuminate both the old and the new. Because of the sometimes strange and awkward dance of old and new together, both are enriched. Without the dance, the riches would not emerge.

The church does not consist of two solitudes, one appreciating the former things and the other anticipating the new that will replace them. There are two energies, to be sure: one searching the past for its stability, wisdom, and heritage; the other scanning the future for new possibilities. When these two realities are acknowledged and affirmed as valuable, they can work together and inform one another. The stability underlying existing patterns can ground and stabilize new initiatives, and the vitality of new initiatives can enliven existing patterns.

As we develop a sharpened awareness of thresholds, we can be sure that our new awareness will serve some who participate in our existing patterns of ministry. As we probe our biblical story within existing patterns of ministry, we can be sure that we will find gifts and resources to serve and illuminate the journeys of those who do not participate in those patterns. As we experiment, we will find riches for both existing patterns and new possibilities.

This accidental outcome, which emerged at St. Cuthbert's as we began to act on what we were learning in The Discovery Project, may be the most important development of all. First, it has invited us to see our current members as people searching, and to take seriously the struggles and celebrations that they embody in our midst. Secondly, because we have evidence of deep spirituality and insights among those who choose not to participate in the life of organized religion, it has helped us within our community to take seriously the spiritual dimension in the lives of our members. Thirdly, the spirituality of non-participants has proved helpful in our approach to worship, to pastoral care, to outreach, and to adult learning within our congregation. The initiatives we take, the learning we experience, and the new insights we entertain in our commitment to those outside church life have begun to strengthen and transform the existing patterns of congregational life.

The marks of the lively historic-cultural church

The implications of Old Churches, New Christians and The Discovery Project are only beginning to emerge for us. We can begin to discern the outlines of a viable identity for historic-cultural churches as we enter the next century. The lively historic-cultural church of the next few decades will

- maintain the stance of servant-teacher towards those around it
- pay careful attention to threshold experiences in the human journey, and focus ministry efforts to serve those who experience them
- take seriously that the church itself is in a liminal state
- listen carefully for the spiritual dimension in the stories of those who are not active in churches
- experiment with new ways of building the connection between lived human experience and the reality of God
- see both existing patterns and new developments as sources of mutual illumination
- be grounded in vital and meaningful worship and learning for its members
- express in worship the real human stories of its members' lives in a thoughtful and authentic way
- emphasize community and relationship over institution and hierarchy
- begin its learning and teaching with the pressing issues and concerns of people's lives

- be a place in which struggle and celebration, rooted in people's experiences both of brokenness and wonder, will find creative and hopeful expression
- be a place in which the gods of the consumer marketplace are challenged with good news of a God who seeks partners in healing the life of the world

A few years ago, in *The Once and Future Church*, Loren Mead concluded that none of us alive will see the "future church." I believe he is right. But by taking seriously the things we can learn from conversations like those in Old Churches, New Christians and The Discovery Project, we can help ensure that there is one. Without such careful listening, the historic-cultural churches will disappear, either by failing or by so effectively imitating others that we become them.

Churches on the Threshold

Whole churches on the quest

Old Churches, New Christians and The Discovery Project are part of a much larger project in the life of the historic-cultural churches. In this larger project, it is not just persons but whole churches who are on a quest. While individuals are seeking meaning and purpose, trying to give expression to their deeply felt desire to contribute and make a difference, churches are seeking relationship and engagement with people with whom we have lost contact. As people work to make sense of the thresholds they encounter, churches stand on a threshold as well. For historic-cultural churches, the familiar patterns of engagement are losing their power, and there is as yet no real fix on what the new patterns will look like. As we seek out the seekers, we have in common with them the uncomfortable but undeniable realization that the very ground under our feet has shifted.

It is as if we were moving from a very familiar room bright with light, whose dimensions and furniture we know and love, into a new room less well-lighted — in fact, downright dim. There's a lot of movement and sound. People are dancing to the music of three bands playing different music simultaneously. In the shadows, we trip over the furniture and bump into strangers, and when we try to dance, we no sooner pick up the beat of one song than it is obliterated by another. It's no wonder we question our reasons for crossing the threshold into this new room. As we look wistfully back through the doorway at the familiar and trustworthy, we might easily forget the hard reality that we were among the last to leave.

When we enter the new room, we find ourselves being asked to think in new ways about church and world. Around us are people asking deep questions of great spiritual significance — variations on the theme, "How am I doing?" They are probing issues of identity, vocation, values, understanding, community. They are writing and reading best-selling business books with words like "stewardship" and "spirit" in the title. In probing the important dimensions of their lives, they experience the tension between struggle and celebration, between wonder and fallibility. They were all around us in the old room, but we didn't see them. In this new space, they are louder and more obvious, the spiritual dimensions of their lives more insistent, and they have absolutely no expectation of us. For while we never much noticed them in the last room, neither did they notice us. But now, sharing this new time and place with them, we might begin to discover that the old story we've carried from room to room with us for four thousand years, first as the people Israel, and then as a people of a new covenant, is about struggle and celebration, about wonder and fallibility, about them as much as about us.

Our leaders now are more like scouts, or spies, than like managers. We look to them not to manage us, but to value our gifts and see what we sometimes cannot see — that our gifts have a contribution to make to life in this strange new world. We look to them not to tell us an old, familiar story, but to raise up the strange hopefulness of the story we thought was familiar, even to equip us to co-author with God a new chapter in the story of purpose, meaning, and hope, the story that allows a fresh wind of spirit to enliven a new world.

It is in the midst of this reality that projects like Old Churches, New Christians and The Discovery Project emerge.

They are not packages to be applied indiscriminately to any and all situations, but a witness to how we can act on our churches' desire to seek the seekers. Their usefulness is not in reproducing them, but in learning from them, and using them as a framework within which to begin that process of engagement.

Serving in new circumstances

The goal of both projects is not to tell the participants anything, but to create a context in which they can address us. The projects seek seekers, not as recruits but as informants, as people who can help us to understand the complex and challenging dimensions of spirituality in the lives of our neighbours, friends, and co-workers.

What we learn from seekers who share the spiritual dimension of their lives with us is the "lay of the land." The land in which they live is today's mission field. Like other generations of missionaries, we find ourselves challenged by an unfamiliar landscape, new customs, shifting priorities. The goal is not, in the first instance, to change those things, but to understand them.

In the neighbourhood of St. Cuthbert's, for example, the school's Christmas concert has become a "holiday concert." The cultural primacy of Christianity has given way to a new and often awkward pluralism, very different from the state of affairs in 1939, the year the school was built. Then, as the plaque outside the school office attests, one member of the school board was a local clergyman. It would not surprise me to find that pattern repeated in many towns and cities in that era. Two institutions, church and school, shared a common cause, and gave mutual support from institution to institution.

It is no longer so. The easy collaboration between educational and religious institutions has come to an end. The holiday concert recognizes students and parents as persons with a variety of different connections, or none at all, to different faith communities. Understanding that the era of mutual institutional support has ended, we face a choice. We can long for its restoration, as many do. Or we can learn how to serve effectively in this new circumstance.

The first option — return to the past — is unattractive, especially for historic-cultural churches, because it leads us into a relationship with our context that is, to one degree or another, hostile. The page will not be turned back. The web of institutional relationships will never be what it used to be. Longing for it will lead to bitterness or frustration, a sense of being blocked by the same society in which we are called to function as servant-teachers.

The second option — learning to serve in new circumstances — is merely difficult! It will help us to remember that, while we are no longer allied with institutions, nor endowed with status by virtue of such an alliance, we can continue to build relationships with persons and with the organizations by which they seek the common good. In fact, set free from the entanglements of power and status, we may begin to appear more sympathetic to those persons and organizations, more trustworthy as servants and partners. We may be more resourceful when our tradition is set free from bondage to status and power. Our tradition is about spirit, hope, and healing. If that was obscured in the past by our symbiosis with power and privilege, it may become clear, useful, and lifegiving now that we have lost that power and privilege.

Embracing the changes demanded by life on the threshold

The issue then is, "Who will change?" The answer is, of course, that everyone will. But the church has an opportunity to retrieve its cultural leadership by embracing both the difficulty and the promise of life on the threshold. The Spirit calls us to begin by listening, that we may understand the landscape in which we seek the seekers. The next step is to ask what we might do differently to secure a hearing for the gospel in this new land. The vitality of the historic-cultural churches depends on our capacity to change, not at the heart of our spirituality, but in the infrastructure of practices by which we render that spirituality accessible to those around us. At the heart of our mission is the same spiritual heritage — compassion, healing, purpose, forgiveness, freedom — which has always been there, and for which so many of our contemporaries yearn. What is clear is that the infrastructure we have constructed to communicate that heritage has become an obstacle rather than a vehicle for communication. In fact, when we look carefully, we find signs of churches that have confused the gift with the infrastructure used to communicate it. We have fallen too much in love with our habits and customs, and too little in love with the gift entrusted to us that we might share it with others. Old Churches, New Christians and The Discovery Project give voice to those who yearn for the gift, but resist the packaging.

When the situation is presented in such clear terms, our responsibility becomes equally clear. The historic-cultural churches are being asked to change the way that we point to God, so that the God to whom we point may become visible, real, and alive to seekers. Part of our responsibility is to understand the organizational life of our churches. But dexterity with the organizational elements of change will not be enough. Woven through the lives of congregations are persons with real and vital attachments to the past, and with deep grief at the passing of patterns that formed and shaped their lives. Leaders who seek to create a hospitable environment for change need to read the congregation's life both on the organizational and on the personal scale, making use of strategies that will honour the reality of structures and of the persons who inhabit those structures.

Organizationally, change begins with dissatisfaction. Somewhere, in almost any congregation, there is a core of dissatisfaction. Perhaps it is focused on size, or on the absence of a particular demographic group: "Where are the young people?" Perhaps there is dissatisfaction with the form of worship, or with music, or preaching. Wherever there is expressed dissatisfaction, there is an impulse towards change. For leaders seeking to support change, dissatisfaction is an opportunity. Not every dissatisfaction will lead necessarily to constructive change. In some forms, dissatisfaction will go no further than complaint. In other cases, it is nostalgic rather than future oriented. But some of the expressions of dissatisfaction will help to create a climate for change.

Dissatisfaction supports change when there is a corresponding vision. Does the absence of young people, for example, result in a vision that includes them, seeks them out, listens to them, and makes room for them in a congregation's common life? Does such a vision grow beyond young people and foster a commitment to real hospitality in the congregation's life? Might a congregation deliberately try to carve out an inviting space for those who find themselves on life's thresholds, and to reach out with companionship and illumination to those who are entering uncertain new lives? Creating a climate hospitable to change means stimulating the sources of vision in a congregation. For while the ordained leader is often the one charged with articulating the vision, he or she is not necessarily its source.

On the other hand, those who advocate change will encounter powerful currents of resistance. Changes in worship patterns, the introduction of new programs, or the appearance of unfamiliar faces in leadership roles often stimulate such resistance. Congregational leaders need to know where resistance is focused and how deep and strong it is. With such knowledge we can find a pathway for innovation that does not stir up strong, early resistance to the idea of change itself.

Organizations such as congregations often resist overarching unified strategies for organizational change. An overarching strategy exposes those who advocate change to resistance from a variety of perspectives. The time necessary to implement such change is so great that dissatisfaction can shift from its original source and become focused on the process of change itself. At the same time, resistance gains a variety of effective leverage points, given the number of changes that need to be strung together in order to effect the overall strategy. While affirming the importance of a simple, clear, and compact vision, some researchers into organizational life advocate quick, small, and incremental changes consistent with the vision. This process of "rapid cycle change" shelters the developmental process from at least some of the resistance that it might encounter, and allows leaders to enjoy and celebrate success in one area without having to defend an overall strategy. At the same time, it allows initiatives to be shaped by the impact of earlier changes, rather than being defined at the beginning of the change process.

Congregations who set out to seek the seekers, then, will encounter a new landscape that will call for change in strategy, priorities, and actions. Leaders in such congregations have responsibility to discern the avenues of change that will be most likely to find acceptance and support in the congregation, beginning their discernment by identifying sources of dissatisfaction and vision in the congregation, and taking into account sources of focused and effective resistance. Such resistance may be based on the heritage and identity of the congregation, and expressed through loyalty of a significant part of the congregation to a particular element of its life. Finally, effective initiatives for change may be more likely to emerge out of "rapid cycle change" strategies, quick, small, and incremental changes aligned with the vision, rather than integrated, overarching strategies for broad change. Many of the changes called for in congregations who set out to connect with seekers will be based on timely, limited initiatives rather than massive planning processes.

But there are likely to be limits in approaching change with timely, limited initiatives. The historic-cultural churches are themselves on a threshold, in a liminal state that is at the same time both threatening and hopeful. If we are to emerge through this threshold as renewed gospel communities, there are important lessons and painful encounters that we cannot avoid.

It is not difficult to see the three-fold pattern being played out in our churches: separation from the way we were as a successful institution in the recent past, entry into a liminal phase in which we adjust to the new reality of our loss of power and prestige, and a return to normal but transformed life. Within this pattern there are two essential tasks: letting the past die, and making space for the new to emerge.

The historic-cultural churches have imbibed a basic cultural attitude that is not part of their own heritage — an overwhelming fear of death. Yet we are experiencing great loss in terms of numbers of adherents and social influence at every level of the church. Getting past our denial into an honest acceptance that we have lost things we have valued is the first step towards experiencing the more healthy emotions of grieving and separation: anger, sorrow, guilt, regret, and yes, gratitude.

Sooner or later, congregational leaders will encounter not just resistance, but grief. Strategies like rapid cycle change will not be enough to answer the reality of loss. Congregations at the threshold of a new millennium will call for wisdom and courage as well as for careful strategic planning from their leaders; for many of them, the new will not be visible until the old has been honoured and grieved. The time will come — and wise leaders will know it when it appears — when the loss must be acknowledged.

If a congregation does successfully let go of its past, then it can begin to cross the threshold towards the new. As it negotiates the threshold, it will experience both excitement and anxiety. The excitement comes out of the opportunity to build a new Christian community full of life and Spirit. To approach the surrounding culture and the seekers who inhabit it without the necessity of defending or rationalizing past structures and relationships will be a heady and life-giving experience. But with those structures and relationships go security and predictability, and their absence will create significant anxiety.

The benefits of this threshold time are reflection and discovery. Once loss has been acknowledged and mourned, it is possible for people to think, pray, and experiment together, so that new expressions of the church can emerge. Leaders are called to hold open the space in which this reflection and discovery can take place. Leading at the threshold means providing security and guarding against manipulation and impatience. A truly new and corporate vision will take time, listening, and patience.

In retrospect, it is clear to me that The Discovery Project came at a critical time in the life of St. Cuthbert's. The congregation I met in 1992 was already engaged in the struggle of seeking the new and relinquishing the old. The leadership of the congregation, including my predecessor, had helped it to come to terms with the passing of a familiar, trusted, and faithful pattern of congregational life.

The Discovery Project was born of a desire to learn and reflect, with the strong hope that we would be led, over time, into a new pattern as church. We had to resist the temptation to use these interviews for recruiting, which would have simply pulled us back into the past. We had to hold open our space and reflect on what we were learning instead of jumping directly into creating programs that we thought might attract the seekers. Our task was discovery, as much about ourselves as about those around us — a discovery that was exciting and uncomfortable. We needed time to let the new emerge.

The Discovery Project is an example of another important aspect of leadership in this phase of change. Although the liminal phase is described in terms of listening and learning and waiting for the new to emerge, there need to be activities to learn from. The creative leader is able to help experiments to happen and to assist the reflective, learning process. He or she also helps with the formation and maintenance of communities within the congregation that are characterized by strong personal bonds and that will be the places in which the most intense learning will occur.

We haven't got a blueprint for the third phase in this process. It's the blueprint everybody wants, so that they can engineer their congregations into the new millennium, without going through the first two phases. There's pain as well as excitement in those phases and there's a lot of uncertainty. We probably want to avoid those things, but we can't. The third phase begins when we start to normalize some of the experiments that we initiated in our liminal, learning time. Perhaps we will find new ways of expressing community in which spiritual issues are kept to the fore; perhaps we will find new ways of worshipping; perhaps we will discover new ways of connecting with people in our neighbourhoods, serving them and nurturing their desire for growth and good living out of the rich loam of the Christian tradition.

But if our commitment to seek the seekers is not informed by recruiting, and makes peace with the continuum of belief and spiritual practices that is our heritage, what is it that identifies us? Without an identity, a discernible character, we run the risk of becoming invisible.

One possible, and promising source of identity for the historic-cultural churches is found in the meeting place of biblical narrative and the voices of Old Churches, New Christians and The Discovery Project. Following Jesus, the servant-teacher whose mission was grounded in costly love, setting free the gifts and hopes of those he encountered, we meet people who yearn to make a difference. We meet people who are searching for sustainable hope and purpose in the tension between struggle and celebration, who ask the question, "How am I doing?" about a number of key dimensions of their lives, dimensions that we understand as spiritual.

Returning to the biblical narrative, we discover, especially in the prophets, a God who is deeply engaged in the life of the world. We discover a God whose passion is not religion but justice, not piety but peace; whose holiness, encountered in the temple, is to be embodied in the world in healing earth's wounds and reconciling earth's creatures.

In light of this dialogue-in-waiting between the God disclosed in the biblical narrative and the church-wary children of

God disclosed in our seeking the seekers, there is a challenge and a promise to tired historic-cultural churches. The challenge is to reclaim our identity as a community in which people are nurtured, challenged, and sustained in their spiritual journey. And the promise is that, as we reclaim that identity, those people will feel their desire to make a difference come to life, and grow in their capacity to love, to serve, to heal, and to renew the world God loves, serves, heals, and renews.

For the historic-cultural churches, the outcome we seek is not successful recruiting towards institutional well-being. It is not a closely defined set of "right" beliefs or "right" expressions of religious experience. It is, at the heart of the matter, people sustained in purpose, meaning, and hope, sustained to be God's partners in the life of the world.

APPENDIX

Resources for
The Discovery Project

Letter of introduction to focus group participants

Thank you for agreeing to come. I want to welcome you, and provide you with an overview of our project. As a church, we hear pretty clearly that people have a deep interest in spirituality. We also hear that for a lot of people, making the connection between spirituality and organized religion is not possible or even desirable.

As a church, though, we have a deep interest in spirituality, too, and we want to be responsible participants in this society, where people are engaged in spiritual searching and exploring. If there are ways we could help foster a connection with people, we want to know what they are. And if there are things we are doing that make that connection difficult or impossible for people to make, we need to know that, too.

That's where you are really important to us. *You* have insights, experiences, and knowledge that we hope to learn from. Our explorations tonight will follow a number of different paths. First, we hope to learn what resources you draw on to sustain you on your spiritual journeys. Second, we hope to learn from you some of the ways that church life could be better organized or lived out in order to be more hospitable to people like you.

A promise: This isn't about convincing you to join the church. It's about hearing from you, listening to you, and being open to your experiences as we think about our church's future.

Interview process for focus groups: facilitator's notes

Preparing for the focus group

You will need
- a good tape recorder with 2 hours of blank tape
- a notebook for your note taking
- workbooks and pens for participants

Try to provide a comfortable environment for the participants. If you are serving refreshments, keep it brief!

Decide in advance which questions you must ask, using which criteria. You have only 80 minutes, and you may not be able to pursue all 7 questions. (Allow 5 minutes for the introduction and 5 minutes for the concluding evaluation.)

Process

Introduce people.
Explain the reason for the focus groups.
Refer to the taping of the interview.
Provide participants with workbooks and pens.
Ensure that what they say will be kept confidential.

Allow sufficient time for introverts to gather their thoughts and make notes.
Ask supplementary questions.
Encourage group interaction.
Make sure people know they can "pass" and are not required to respond to questions if they don't want to.

Questions

Note that the introduction to each question is for the interviewers. It gives some direction about what to listen for and provides suggestions for follow-up questions.

1. *Purpose: To discover what participants mean by spirituality, and what associations that word conveys to them. Lay out the pictures.*
Think of the word spirituality; does it have positive or negative associations for you? Now choose one of these pictures which may convey to you something of what you mean by spirituality. (Discussion and exploration — images, symbols, anything to do with God, etc.)

2. *Purpose: To find out what unchurched people "treasure." Who agrees or denies that such treasure exists.*
Take a moment and list all the things you value in life. You may wish to consider personal experience and community life.

Pause
Now choose two things you value most and couldn't live without.

Share & discuss
Do you think that your most important values are affirmed or denied in our society? Where do you find support for them?

3. *Purpose: To find out to what extent unchurched people wish to make a difference in the world, and for whom.*
We will all be remembered, even if only briefly, when our lives are over. What would you like to be remembered for? What difference do you want your life to make in this world?

Who do you want to remember you?

4. Purpose: To discover levels and instances of dissonance and satisfaction with personal goals.
What is an accomplishment in your recent life that you take a great deal of satisfaction from? How did you celebrate that accomplishment, or how did you express this satisfaction?

What is an issue or concern that you haven't really resolved yet? What do you think you need in order to resolve it?

Suggestion for follow-up question
What would you be disappointed not to have accomplished in the next five years?

5. Purpose: To find out participants' views of spirituality. Does spirituality develop? What helps or hinders spiritual growth? What actions do people take (e.g., quiet times for thinking, discussion groups, music, reading, hiking, volunteering)? What actions do people they admire take? What language do people use to speak of spirituality?
What in your view is most necessary or important for the health and development of the human spirit?

What hinders or destroys this development? What helps it? How much control do you think you have in your own development?

6. Purpose: To discover attitudes to the church, both positive and negative, and how the church could connect with unchurched people.
If you were on the board of (insert name of church) and were discussing how best this church could make a significant difference to the lives of people like you, what would be your one recommendation?

7. *Purpose: To evaluate the focus group experience, to fill out the consent forms, and to inform participants of the opportunity to attend an information session.*
We would like to take the last five minutes to give you the opportunity to evaluate our time together. Have you any comments on how you felt about our discussion?

Ask participants to fill in their forms, and invite them to the information session. Close with thanks.

Workbook for participants

Thank you for agreeing to participate in this focus group. We value your insights, experiences, and reflections. At the same time we need to reassure you that, while what you say will matter, you won't be identified in any way. The names of participants will remain anonymous. We do ask you to fill in the following information, so that we can compare responses from group to group. Please use the attached worksheet for those parts of our process that call for list making and written notes. These, too, will be kept anonymous, but will be important as we learn as much as we can from you.

Age _____ Sex _____ Marital status _____

Ages of children _____

Ethnic origin _____

Occupation _____

Type of music you listen to most _____

Leisure activities _____

Level of formal education _____

Questions

1. Reflect on the "Images of Spirituality"

2. List the things you value (identify with an X the two you couldn't live without).

3. What you want to be remembered for

4. Significant accomplishments and unresolved issues

5. The health and development of the human spirit

6. What would you like to see the church doing?

7. Evaluating our time together

Additional comments

Consent form for focus group participants

I consent to having my written and spoken comments used within the research context of The Discovery Focus Groups. I understand that I will not be identified by name, and that the taped transcription and notes will be seen only by the focus group leaders.

Name _____

Telephone _____

I would like to be contacted and invited to an information session

---

Letter inviting facilitators to feedback session

Dear
Thank you for the work you have done for The Discovery Project, interviewing people in focus groups. I am writing to ask you to come to a meeting, so that we may begin the process of discovering and developing themes, issues, and concerns you have experienced with the focus group participants.

In preparation for this meeting, you might wish to reflect on the following questions.

1. What did you hear that felt familiar and comfortable to you?

2. What themes, ideas, or concerns surprised you?

3. What is the most interesting thing you learned from the participants?

4. What things in the conversation do you think our church would find the hardest to respond to?

5. Having spent time with the focus group participants, what one thing would you wish could be different in their lives and in the way we gather for church?

Please let me know if you are unable to attend the meeting.

As always,

Bibliography

Ammerman, Nancy. "Culture and Identity in the Congregation," *Studying Congregations: A New Handbook*. Edited by Nancy Ammerman et al. Nashville: Abingdon Press, 1998.

Anderson, Herbert, and Robert Foley. *Mighty Stories, Dangerous Rituals: Weaving Together the Human and the Divine*. San Francisco: Jossey-Bass, 1997.

Bridges, William. *Transitions: Making Sense of Life's Changes*. Addison-Wesley Publishing Co., 1980.

Fowler, James. *Stages of Faith: The Psychology of Human Development and the Quest for Meaning*. San Francisco: Harper and Rowe, 1981.

Kegan, Robert. *In Over Our Heads: The Mental Demands of Modern Life*. Cambridge, Ma: Harvard Unversity Press, 1994.

Mead, Loren. *The Once and Future Church: Reinventing the Congregation for a New Mission Frontier*. Washington, DC: Alban Institute, 1991.

Roof, Wade Clark. *A Generation of Seekers: The Spiritual Journeys of the Baby Boom Generation*. Harper San Francisco, Division of HarperCollins, 1993.

Suchocki, Marjorie. "Friends in the Family," *Christian Identity and Theological Education*. Edited by Joseph C. Hough and Barbara Wheeler. Chico, Ca: Scholars Press, 1985.

Victor, Turner. *The Ritual Process: Structure and Anti-Structure*. Chicago: Aldine, 1969.

Yeats, William Butler. "The Second Coming," *Collected Poems of William Butler Yeats*. London: MacMillan, 1965, p. 210.

About the Authors

PAUL MACLEAN is the executive director of Potentials, a Canadian ecumenical centre for the development of ministry and congregations. He has had a lifelong interest in and love of congregations, and through Potentials has helped many congregations with vision planning, research, and facilitation. Paul has theological degrees from Toronto and the Episcopal Divinity School in Cambridge, Massachusetts. Before founding Potentials, he served as an Anglican priest in parishes in Canada and the UK, and then on the national staff of the Anglican Church for education and congregational development. He coauthored *Sharing the Banquet: Liturgical Renewal in Your Parish*. Paul is married to Sally-Beth, and they have three adult children.

Currently in his eighth year as incumbent of St. Cuthbert's Anglican Church in Toronto, MICHAEL THOMPSON is a graduate of Huron College, University of Western Ontario (BA), and of Trinity College, University of Toronto (MDiv and DMin). Ordained in the Diocese of Edmonton, where he served in two parishes over five years, he also spent four years as Dean of Men at Trinity College. For several years he served as a member and subsequently as chair of the board of the magazine *The Practice of Ministry in Canada*, in which his articles and editorials have become a popular feature. He is married and lives with his wife, Deborah Tregunno, their three children, and Maggie the dog in a home that's bigger than it looks.

Enquiries about Old Churches, New Christians and The Discovery Project should be addressed to:

Potentials: A Canadian Centre for the Development of Ministry and Congregations
761 Queen St. West
Suite 309
Toronto, ON
M6J 1G1

phone 416-504-3664
fax 416-504-3765
e-mail potentials@tap.net

Paul MacLean, executive director
Janet Marshall Eibner, staff consultant